The Catholic Church
and the Struggle for
Racial Justice

The **CATHOLIC CHURCH** and the **STRUGGLE** for **RACIAL JUSTICE**

A Prophetic Call

MATHEW KAPPADAKUNNEL
FOREWORD BY
JOSEPH BROWN, SJ

Paulist Press
New York / Mahwah, NJ

Scripture texts in this work are taken from the *New American Bible, revised edition* © 2010, 1991, 1986, 1970 Confraternity of Christian Doctrine, Washington, D.C., and are used by permission of the copyright owner. All Rights Reserved. No part of the New American Bible may be reproduced in any form without permission in writing from the copyright owner.

Cover image by albund / Depositphotos, Inc.
Cover and book design by Lynn Else

Copyright © 2024 by Mathew Kappadakunnel

All rights reserved. No part of this publication may be reproduced, stored in a retrieval system, or transmitted in any form or by any means, electronic, mechanical, photocopying, recording, scanning, or otherwise, without either the prior written permission of the Publisher, or authorization through payment of the appropriate percopy fee to the Copyright Clearance Center, Inc., www.copyright.com. Requests to the Publisher for permission should be addressed to the Permissions Department, Paulist Press, permissions@paulistpress.com.

Library of Congress Cataloging-in-Publication Data
Names: Kappadakunnel, Mathew, author.
Title: The Catholic church and the struggle for racial justice : a prophetic call / Mathew Kappadakunnel ; foreword by Joseph Brown, SJ.
Description: New York ; Mahwah : Paulist Press, [2024] | Summary: "This book is an invitation to respond to the prophetic call, stemming from baptism, to promote the dignity of all people based on the belief that each person is created in the image of God, particularly those who suffer racial injustice"—Provided by publisher.
Identifiers: LCCN 2023030625 (print) | LCCN 2023030626 (ebook) | ISBN 9780809156481 (paperback) | ISBN 9780809188093 (ebook)
Subjects: LCSH: Race relations—Catholic Church. | Racism—Religious aspects—Catholic Church. | Social justice—Religious aspects—Catholic Church. | United States—Race relations.
Classification: LCC BX1795.R33 K36 2024 (print) | LCC BX1795.R33 (ebook) | DDC 261.8/3—dc23/eng/20231130
LC record available at https://lccn.loc.gov/2023030625
LC ebook record available at https://lccn.loc.gov/2023030626

ISBN 978-0-8091-5648-1 (paperback)
ISBN 978-0-8091-8809-3 (e-book)

Published by Paulist Press
997 Macarthur Boulevard
Mahwah, New Jersey 07430
www.paulistpress.com

Printed and bound in the
United States of America

CONTENTS

Foreword vii
   Joseph Brown, SJ

Preface xi

Acknowledgments xv

Part 1: Our Church's Call to Racial Justice 1
  1. Introduction: A Baptismal Call to Prophetic Witness 3
  2. The Heresy of Racism and the *Imago Dei* 11
  3. Racism: The Antithesis of the Catholicity of the Church 18

Part 2: Racism and a Divided Church 31
  4. A House of Divided Bishops Cannot Stand against Racism 33
  5. Empty Words and Empty Promises 44
  6. Restoring and Rebuilding the Divided House 64
  7. The U.S. Church in the Third Millennium 80
  8. A Coalition of Clergy and Laity against Social Justice 85

Part 3: Evasion and Admission of the Sin of Racism 103

9. The Anti-Social Justice Bogeymen 105

10. Black Lives Are Being Aborted—and Not Just in
    the Womb 115

11. Bridging the Divide: A Call to Unity 123

Notes 131

FOREWORD

What this book announces to all who have the humility and courage (two components of any true act of heroism) to read it all the way through is one of the most basic truths of the revelations of Jesus the Christ: in the Kingdom of God, there are no strangers, no *others*, no aliens—only our neighbors. With each statement of judgement, challenge, and exhortation, Matt Kappadakunnel brings prophetic truth to the reader. "We must love one another or die." Kappadakunnel's voice is prophetic in the most basic sense: the authority of his writing comes from his raw humility to speak from his experience. His story of his search for spiritual insight and cultural honesty compels him to call his readers to discern as deeply as possible what each of us understands about what Church *should* be. And Kappadakunnel gathers a "cloud of witnesses" (Heb 12:1) to confirm and support his vision of what *church must be* if the new covenant is to prevail within the community of believers who identify as Roman Catholics in the United States.

The Catholic Church and the Struggle for Racial Justice: A Prophetic Call. The starting point of this challenging work is the author's painstaking effort to define the terms by which Catholics should profess their faith, their "kingdom identity"; and to also define the realities that keep the vision of some so far out of reach as to be an indictment of the hypocrisy that too often marks the Catholic Church in the United States. Kappadakunnel provides a review of how formerly persecuted "nonwhite" European immigrants in the nineteenth and early twentieth centuries followed the description of what James Baldwin called "the price of the ticket":

> The price the white American paid for his ticket was to become white—and, in the main, nothing more than that, or, as he was to insist, nothing less. This incredibly limited not to say dimwitted ambition has choked many a human being to death here: and this, I contend, is because the white American has never accepted the real reasons for his journey. I know very well that my ancestors had no desire to come to this place: but neither did the ancestors of the people who became white and who require of my captivity a song.[1]

The Catholic Church and the Struggle for Racial Justice shines the light on the hierarchical authorities of the U.S. Roman Catholic Church, whose ancestors belonged to the groups who were persecuted upon arrival with violence and racial discrimination and whose efforts to escape such injustices brought them to their goal: eventual assimilation into "mainstream" society. And the rewards for assimilation are also detailed with a thoroughness that will challenge readers to the core of their faith. Clerical leaders who argue against efforts of Black Americans to demand security, safety, respect, and justice are held up in the light of the author's investigations. There are also forceful, detailed critiques of the Eternal Word Television Network, the Napa Institute, the Knights of Columbus, and the intertwined forces that support each of these organizations and several other calmly and proudly "conservative" wealthy influ-

Foreword

encers who are shaping one dominating side of the "Catholic culture wars in the United States."

Another of the accomplishments of this prophetic challenge is to read the United States Conference of Catholic Bishops' letters on racism and confront the fact that actions do not meet the rhetoric. It is Kappadakunnel's contention that most of the U.S. Roman Catholic Church leadership continues to falter in living up to the call of catholicity, but especially with regard to standing with the racially marginalized. It is by virtue of the gift of his humility that he also provides exceptions to this tendency. The bishops who have chosen to "wade in the water" and confront the sin of racism in the United States are named and confirmed throughout this book.

Finally, Matt Kappadakunnel presents a radical reading of the implications of the new covenant: Who is the Good Samaritan, the robbers, those who bypass the victim? Who is truly the *neighbor* who must be loved completely, without limit? What will be the rewards, on earth, for adhering to this radical revision of what too many of us have allowed to become a false "gospel truth"? Racism is a sin, we are told. A fatal, mortal wounding of all who are victims. And we all are victims. Which means that we all are bound together. And love is the source of hope, for reconciliation and healing. That all may be one....

What Martin Luther King Jr. said in his famous speech to the Southern Christian Leadership Conference in 1967 can be generously poured out as a blessing upon this book and its author:

> We still need some Paul Revere of conscience to alert every hamlet and every village of America that revolution is still at hand. Yes, we need a chart; we need a compass; indeed, we need some North Star to guide

us into a future shrouded with impenetrable uncertainties.

Go forward, reader; go forward. We have a guide who has survived the past and brings us the hope of how we can make it to the other shore, no matter how "troubled the waters."

Joseph A. Brown, SJ, PhD
Professor, Director, School of Africana & Multicultural Studies
Southern Illinois University Carbondale

PREFACE

A voice proclaims:
In the wilderness prepare the way of the Lord!
Make straight in the wasteland a highway for
  our God!
—Isaiah 40:3

The year 2020 opened my eyes to a prophetic call, rooted in Baptism, to support and defend the racially marginalized.

For several years, I seem to have been asleep while Black lives were being unjustly murdered. While in the background I was aware of the Black Lives Matter Global Organization and its movement, I really didn't pay much attention to it. In fact, I favored "staying in my lane." However, when the untimely death of George Floyd occurred, I believe God called me to start *getting in God's lane* of seeing the harm being done to Black and Brown people through the Trinity's lens and to draw near to the racially marginalized.

I began reading books such as Ibram X. Kendi's *How to Be an Antiracist*, which gave me greater awareness of how I have been socialized with racist beliefs, as well as discovering how racist beliefs were being promulgated in the Catholic Church.

In 2020, I first began writing articles in response to statements issued by certain prelates that seemed aimed at dissuading Catholics from participating in racial justice movements. I believe that it was the Spirit using my baptismal call as prophet to boldly speak out against such statements. The Holy Spirit was not going to let me be deluded by hierarchical messaging, and the Spirit wanted to ensure that others might not be deluded as well. Thus began more than a year of spontaneous, freelance writing.

I do not believe I am the only one called to proclaim the dignity of the racially marginalized. This, in fact, is inherent in our baptismal call. We are created in the *Imago Dei* and are called to reverence the *Imago Dei* in others. Embedded in this call is to defend those who are treated as if they were not created in the *Imago Dei*. Rather, these individuals become casualties of what Pope Francis labels "throwaway culture" (*Evangelii Gaudium* 53), but more specifically they are harmed by the *sin of racism*.

While our Church upholds that racism is a sin, the actions of certain bishops, clergy, and laity suggest the opposite. Therefore, this book offers a reminder that racial justice is not a secular movement but a call for all the baptized.

In part 1, I exhort that we are *all* called to witness to the *Imago Dei* in *all* people, and thereby be truly *pro-life*. Racism is not only a sin but a heresy, which denies the *Imago Dei* by suggesting those who are of certain ethnicities are inferior and thus not created in the likeness of God. In addition, drawing from Henri de Lubac's *Catholicism*, I discuss his citations from the Church fathers, particularly the Eastern fathers, which uphold the universality and multicultural basis of the Church. In light of this, racism is the antithesis to the catholicity of the Church.

In part 2, I outline the divisions in the U.S. Church regarding racial justice. Not only do I highlight members of the clergy who do not support the dignity of the racially marginalized, but organizations such as the Napa Institute and EWTN that favor right-wing talking points over the gospel call to love our neighbor—*every* neighbor.

In part 3, I discuss some of the diversions that aim to lead

Preface

Catholics away from racial justice, namely, the Marxism/Critical Race Theory bogeymen, and the "All Lives Matter" and "Blue Lives Matter" fallacies. I call on Catholics to reflect on how racism can be considered a "mortal" sin, including but not limited to the abortion of Black lives—*not just in the womb.*

Much of the discourse is focused on anti-Black racism mainly because this seems to be the area that the U.S. Church struggles with the most. For example, Church leaders can be vocal when it comes to migrants and refugees. However, no Church leader seems to have stood up to a presidential candidate who referred to Mexicans as those who bring drugs and crime and are "rapists"[1] who "infest"[2] the United States.

As a Catholic born to Indian immigrants, I am saddened by how U.S. Church leaders blatantly disfavor certain ethnicities. As I was growing up, I often felt like an outsider in any Catholic parish, when the land my parents came from, Kerala, India, is home to the early Christians converted by the preaching of the Apostle Thomas. I have an ancient ancestral claim to the Catholic faith that no one can deny.

While the Church and its leaders, whether clergy or prominent laypeople, undermine the mission and identity of the Church by being complicit with racial injustice and not taking an active stand for the racially marginalized, we, the nameless Catholics in the pews, have a power and a call from on high. God wants to use us to lead the Church to its intended catholicity and to remove from it the harmful sin of racism, often manifest in white supremacy. God wants to use us as a healing balm to alleviate the division in the Body of Christ.

Let us be the voice crying out to the Church to prepare the Way of the Lord—a Way that promotes inclusion and the dignity of all human beings and seeks to defend and protect all of those harmed by the sin and heresy of racism.

ACKNOWLEDGMENTS

First, I would like to give thanks to the Holy Trinity, God's community of love, for giving me the courage to write on such a challenging and controversial topic.

For those who don't know me, I am not a "rock-the-boat" kind of person, however the Holy Spirit inspired me to rock the Barque of Peter. The Spirit revealed to me, through the tragic death of George Floyd, that I cannot be silent in the face of racial injustice. It is Christ they persecute in the form of Black and Brown people, along with my Asian American/Pacific Islander brothers and sisters.

My wife, Bry, was a strong source of encouragement as I began writing, particularly in terms of taking an active stand against racism. Since we met in 2014, she has continually encouraged me to find a way to get involved in the Church. While nothing at a parish level inspired me, the Spirit called me to this work at a time when parishes were closed due to COVID-19, and by the power of online media, the Spirit gave me words that have been read across the globe.

I said yes to the Spirit's calling in this regard because of my two young children, Matteo and Giovanni. By the grace of God, I wish to be for them the father that they so truly deserve, which includes modeling for them the call from Christ to love every neighbor.

I would also like to thank my father, mother, and two sisters. I was introduced to my Catholic faith through my family, and while I resisted embracing my Indian and Syro-Malabar identity in my youth, in my adulthood I learned to appreciate my Indian Christian heritage and my Brown skin. While my long last name and skin color have been a source of ridicule over the course of my life, it is this very sting that the Spirit used to draw me with concern for the racially marginalized. God calls broken, wounded healers to this ministry.

I also want to thank the Catholic educators who taught me, including Rina Ngo, David Kristoff, Donna Brennan, Cathy Urbigkeit, and Dr. Todd Salzman, along with the priests of St. Peter Chanel in Hawaiian Gardens, California, staffed by members of the Oblates of the Virgin Mary.

I want to thank the Jesuits as well. Although I have had a mix of positive and negative experiences with the order, having spent more than three years in formation, my experiences of Ignatian spirituality before, during, and after my time in the Society of Jesus taught me how to find God in daily life and especially in the marginalized. My experiences working with the underprivileged in South Texas and Honduras, with the mentally handicapped in L'Arche, and with the sick and dying in the Bronx taught me that not only is Christ close to those who suffer, but he is present in those who suffer.

I am grateful for all the publications and editors I have worked with since 2020. It has been a privilege to share my reflections to a variety of audiences while growing as a writer in the process. I am indebted to Rebecca Bratten Weiss for taking the time to support and encourage me as a writer, and most importantly to help me grow as a writer. I wish to thank Robert Ellsberg for giving me the initial guidance that resulted in me taking the bold step to write this manuscript.

Without Paulist Press, this book would have never materialized. I am immensely grateful to Donna Crilly for her open-

Acknowledgments

ness to my submission and to Paulist Press for taking a chance on me and believing in this message.

I also want to thank Olga Segura, Gloria Purvis, Tia Noelle Pratt, Shannen Dee Williams, Bryan Massingale, and the cofounders and contributors of *Black Catholic Messenger*. Your words and your witness have made an indelible imprint on how I see the call to racial justice as deeply embedded in the Catholic faith.

Austin Ruse became an instrument of the Lord to teach me to engage with those I disagree with. I want to thank Austin for his cooperation and friendship.

Finally, I wish to thank John Horn, SJ, for serving as my spiritual director and friend for years.

May the Holy Trinity lead us to the divine communion God so desires for us, a communion that cannot be experienced without recognizing that each and every person, regardless of race, has been created in the image of God (see Gen 1:27).

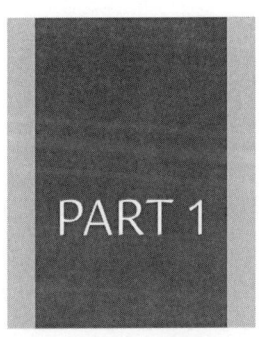

OUR CHURCH'S CALL TO RACIAL JUSTICE

1

INTRODUCTION

A Baptismal Call to Prophetic Witness

More than twenty years ago, I read *Listen, Prophets!* by George Maloney, SJ. This book centered on contemplative and charismatic spirituality and focused on the prophetic vocation embedded within baptism. At that time, I equated prophecy with the charismatic gift, one used to provide a word of knowledge to a person or a group. In my faith formation, I had never learned that the Holy Spirit can inspire the gift of prophecy to respond to injustice, exhibited by bold witnesses such as Dorothy Day.

Back then, I considered social justice the responsibility of nonprofit organizations, whereas I felt called to prayer and to telling people about Jesus. I believed these two callings to be distinct—an either/or as opposed to a both/and. I didn't realize at that time that a deep love for Jesus, instilled in a healthy spirituality, leads one to go where Jesus is and to be with the ones Jesus is with. These, I learned, are the outcasts, the rejected, and the marginalized.

THE CATHOLIC CHURCH AND THE STRUGGLE FOR RACIAL JUSTICE

In my twenties, I did not think I was called to work with the poor. I haughtily viewed clergy who did as "social workers with collars." In August of 2009 I entered the Society of Jesus, and that November I made the life-changing thirty-day Spiritual Exercises. During this time of prayer and direction, I encountered Christ, not just in the chapel but in my experiences. I reflected on the times I was with the homebound or was leading a prayer in a school setting, and I experienced Jesus being there with me, guiding me toward those who desired ministry. I encountered the Jesus in the Gospel accounts who taught me how to live the gospel in my everyday context.

Following the long retreat, I had multiple experiences of ministry that allowed me to experience Christ in poor parishes, amid the dying and mourning family members, in the mentally handicapped, and those living in the Global South. My most eye-opening experience was in encountering those from south of the U.S. border who sought entrance but were turned away. At the time, I had a limited view on immigration. I believed that those who come to the United States illegally are criminals. Why couldn't they come through the legal route as my parents did?

As a Jesuit novice, I met real people who were escaping real dangers.

In 2010, on the Mexican side of Nogales, I spent time with a Catholic initiative called *El Comedor* (the "dining room"). This was a place for people who had been turned away from the U.S. border, where they could receive food, care, and compassion. When I met these people face-to-face, the names, faces, and stories of those trying to emigrate to the United States suddenly became real. These were not opportunists seeking to benefit from U.S. welfare and social services. The people I met were desperate, trying to escape treacherous circumstances that threatened their lives, their safety, and their families.

I became aware of the hardness of heart that formed my old beliefs. I realized they were not "those people," they were

Introduction

God's people, and therefore they were my people. I could no longer judge those who crossed the border seeking a better life. I was filled with the graces of compassion and understanding. This brought me closer to the Lord, as my heart of stone became transformed into a heart of flesh (see Ezek 36:26).

As Gustavo Gutiérrez once noted, "The poor and marginalized have a deep-rooted conviction that no one is interested in their lives and misfortunes."[1] When we overlook the poor and marginalized, we completely miss Christ. Thus, the people at *El Comedor* taught me to find Christ and to stay with him. They were instrumental in transforming my stony heart into flesh and enabled my eyes to see anew. When we encounter the marginalized, we allow God to change us forever.

A year later, I spent three months in Honduras. Every day, I heard of both locals and foreigners being assaulted at gunpoint. I also met people who had lost a loved one. Some were murdered, some were malnourished, and some drank and used drugs too much. What became clear to me, however, was that people were leaving Honduras, going up through Mexico to enter the United States, because they knew death would come knocking at their door. These people embarked on this risky and expensive journey because they were no longer safe in their own homes and in their own country. Through these experiences in Nogales and Honduras, Christ transformed my heart. My vocation became linked to the marginalized. The migrant turned away from the border and the Honduran struggling to make it to the next day became living icons of Jesus.

My experience of the Exercises taught me to be with people who are suffering and become sensitive to how Christ feels toward these people and their situation. I learned, by the grace of God, what Ignatius notes in the Exercises as *sentir*: to feel what Jesus is feeling, regarding a person, a group of people, or a circumstance. Another word for this is having intimate, interior knowledge of Christ, which is found in his Sacred Heart. To feel rejection with the migrant and fear with the Central American escaping danger is to know Christ.

Through these pivotal experiences, I learned that social justice ministry is not simply something for priests with collars and nonprofit organizations. All the baptized are called to draw near to the Sacred Heart of Jesus and to reflect this love to all people, particularly those the Heart of Christ calls us to. As the Psalmist proclaims, "The Lord is close to the broken hearted" (Ps 34:19). We must also be near the marginalized, those broken in spirit due to injustice—not only near them, but fighting alongside them against the injustice that holds them captive.

While I left the Society of Jesus in November 2012, I took with me the experience of the Sacred Heart and the call to be with and love the marginalized. The migrant and the Honduran burned within me the image of Christ and God's deep care for those our society deems the least. Even though life with a job in finance was vastly different from the lives of the people I met south of the U.S. border, they forever changed my relationship to God and my understanding of the Christian vocation.

Fast forward to 2020. I thought I was a good Catholic. I went to Mass on Sundays, I prayed occasionally, dedicated time to spiritual reading, attended regular spiritual direction and confession, and participated in retreats and ongoing faith formation. Additionally, I had my oldest child baptized, and I brought him to Mass every Sunday. However, as can happen to all of us, I was in a rut and didn't know it.

Cue the pandemic, cue the premature death of George Floyd—my world shook. How can a police officer remorselessly place his knee on the neck of an unarmed man, leaving him dead? Sadness flooded my heart. I became aware of the callousness American society exhibits toward Black persons and people of color. While society permits racism despite the gains of the civil rights era and the growth of diversity in the United States, my Catholic faith taught otherwise. Amid the cognitive

Introduction

dissonance of realizing that I was not living in a post-racial society, I turned to my faith for answers. In doing so, my first thought was that surely the bishops would speak out against injustice. Sadly, those I considered heroes in the Church proved to be tone deaf and looked the other way.

The blessing in disguise of these episcopal missteps is that they awakened in me my baptismal call to be *prophet*. At baptism, we are anointed with chrism, and incorporated into Christ who is anointed priest, prophet, and king (CCC, 1241). Like Christ, we are also called by our baptism to be priest, prophet, and king. While it had been nearly forty years since my baptism, the Spirit stirred within me an awakening to be a prophetic voice that cries out against the racial injustice prevalent to and persisting in this day.

A *prophet* is sent by God to a group of people and delivers God's message to them. United with Christ, the baptized assent like the prophet Isaiah, "Here I am, send me!" (Isa 6:8), promulgating to the world that Christ came to give us abundant life (John 10:10). As prophets, the baptized are called to proclaim the good news, God's gratuitous and saving love, but we are also called to deliver a message that promotes *justice*.

The prophet Isaiah is an excellent example of this. He shares this message of justice from God:

> Is this not, rather, the fast that I choose:
>   releasing those bound unjustly,
>   untying the thongs of the yoke;
> Setting free the oppressed,
>   breaking off every yoke?
> Is it not sharing your bread with the hungry,
>   bringing the afflicted and the homeless into your house;
> Clothing the naked when you see them,
>   and not turning your back on your own flesh?
>   (Isa 58:6–7)

Here, Isaiah says that the pious act of fasting is empty if it does not lead us to offer the food that we forego to the one who goes without. Our faith in God is incomplete if it does not lead us to love all of God's people and to express that love, especially to those who are oppressed or lacking in any way.

Another notable example of a prophet called by God to promote justice is Óscar Romero, saint and martyr. While archbishop of San Salvador, Romero experienced a call from God to recognize and respond to the affliction of the poor. Precipitating this call was the murder of his good friend, Rutilio Grande, SJ, on March 12, 1977, three weeks into Romero's episcopacy. Fr. Grande was an outspoken defender of the poor. Grande's murder ushered Romero into advocacy for the poor amid a right-wing military dictatorship, resulting in the archbishop's own death while celebrating Mass three years after the murder of Grande.

While not all of us might be called to be priests and bishops, God calls every baptized person a child of the Kingdom, with an inheritance and a duty to proclaim the gospel. Regardless of our circumstances, every one of us can work to liberate captives and uplift the oppressed, but living out a prophetic vocation is not without cost. We might not become martyrs, but taking a stand against injustice invites opposition and consequences. People we have considered friends, acquaintances at the parish, and even family members might turn against us.

I know of a family who had been highly esteemed by their wealthy, conservative faith community. However, once they expressed their support for migrants seeking to enter the United States through the southern border, and their opposition to a presidential administration that demonized them, the pastor suddenly dropped them from the parish board and the community alienated them. This was a painful blow to this family, as they felt betrayed by their own parish.

Introduction

I also know of Catholic writers and activists who are bombarded with hate-filled messages in their inboxes and on social media. The toxic sting from anonymous accounts using Latin phrases and profile pictures of holy images has lasting mental, spiritual, and psychological effects. It is striking that the opposition to this prophetic work comes not from Satanic or non-Christian sources but from people in our very own Church. This type of repudiation, especially when coming from Church hierarchy, can be devastating.

Thus, the prophetic call coincides with the call to suffer. The Spirit who calls us is also the one who sustains us, so that we can proclaim like St. Paul that we might be cast down, but not destroyed (see 2 Cor 4:9). To be a prophet is not only a testament of faith, but it tests our faith. In the end, the persecution experienced for working for justice allows us to shed that which did not help us grow closer to God, such as esteem from our parish, so that we may be transformed into Christ, who is present in all the marginalized.

I did not expect God to call me to write in defense of the racially oppressed following the murder of George Floyd, but the fire of the Holy Spirit would not allow me to stay silent. I had seen priests and bishops look the other way, and it was a disservice to Christ and his Church to keep silent. Like the Samaritan in the famous parable, Christ was calling me to radically love my neighbor by advocating for justice for those whose spirits have been beaten and robbed by those who have attacked them for their race. In the process of responding to Christ's invitation, I experienced trinitarian love that transformed me to be an instrument of God's message for justice to the racially oppressed in the present.

As we begin this journey together, ask our Lord how God is calling you to set the captives free. God has equipped you to be a prophet. I know this deep in my bones, otherwise the

Spirit would not have led you to this book. Ask God to give you the strength to embrace the suffering that comes with a prophetic calling. Trust that God's Spirit is with you, sustaining you amid suffering, and proclaiming in and through your very being God's message of salvation for the oppressed, particularly those who are harmed due to their race.

2
THE HERESY OF RACISM AND THE *IMAGO DEI*

God of justice,
In your wisdom you create all people in your image,
    without exception.
Through your goodness, open our eyes to see the
    dignity,
beauty, and worth of every human being.
Open our minds to understand that all your
    children are
brothers and sisters in the same human family.
Open our hearts to repent of racist attitudes,
    behaviors, and
speech that demean others.
Open our ears to hear the cries of those wounded
    by racial
discrimination, and their passionate appeals for
    change.
Strengthen our resolve to make amends for past
    injustices
and to right the wrongs of history.

THE CATHOLIC CHURCH AND THE STRUGGLE FOR RACIAL JUSTICE

And fill us with courage that we might seek to heal wounds,
build bridges, forgive and be forgiven, and establish peace
and equality for all in our communities.
In Jesus's name we pray.
Amen.[1]

A fundamental tenet of the Christian faith is that all human beings—regardless of race, skin color, gender, or sexual orientation—are created in the image of God (see Gen 1:27). From the beginning, and in the beginning of the Sacred Scriptures, humans have been stamped with the divine image, the *Imago Dei*. Not only was this belief deeply held in the beginning of the Divine Word but among those in the early Church. The *Imago Dei* was paramount for the Church fathers. St. Irenaeus states in his famous text *Against Heresies*,

> Now God shall be glorified in His handiwork, fitting it so as to be conformable to, and modeled after, His own Son. For by the hands of the Father, that is by the Son and the Holy Spirit, man, and not [merely] a part of man, was made in the likeness of God. (5, 6, I)

The Trinity molded all humans from the form of Christ. Therefore, by faith we can see Jesus in the Black woman, the Asian man, the Muslim refugee, and the Sikh child. We need to let go of any bias within us that prevents us from seeing the Holy Spirit revealed in certain people. No person bears more or less of God's likeness; each of us fully and completely bears the *Imago Dei*. Our God-given dignity is irrefutable. Nothing we can do, and no aspect of who we are, can diminish this.

In commenting on the Church fathers regarding the *Imago Dei*, Henri de Lubac writes,

The Heresy of Racism and the *Imago Dei*

> Thus the unity of the Mystical Body of Christ, a supernatural unity, supposes a previous natural unity, the unity of the human race. So the Fathers of the Church, in their treatment of grace and salvation, kept constantly before them this Body of Christ, and in dealing with the creation were not content only to mention the formation of individuals, the first man and the first woman, but delighted to contemplate God creating humanity as a whole.[2]

Racism, on the other hand, is a sin against the *Imago Dei*, denying the God-given dignity of certain races and peoples. Not only is this an injustice, but it is also a denial of God, whose image is borne by the racially marginalized, a denial of the Body of Christ that is made up of persons from every race, and a denial of the Catholic faith that upheld in its early inception the dignity of all people.

In the National Conference of Catholic Bishops' pastoral letter *Brothers and Sisters to Us* (1979), the bishops offer a detailed explanation of the sin of racism with respect to the *Imago Dei*:

> Racism is a sin: a sin that divides the human family, blots out the image of God among specific members of that family, and violates the fundamental human dignity of those called to be children of the same Father. Racism is the sin that says some human beings are inherently superior and others essentially inferior because of races. It is the sin that makes racial characteristics the determining factor for the exercise of human rights. It mocks the words of Jesus: "Treat others the way you would have them treat you" (Mt 7:12). Indeed, racism is more than a disregard for the words of Jesus; it is a denial of the truth of the dignity of each human being revealed by the mystery of the Incarnation.[3]

Yet how often do we hear from the pulpit about the sin of racism? How often does a parish reconciliation service highlight the need to reflect on how the sin of racism has pervaded one's life? How often are people confessing the sin of racism? The events of 2020 and beyond suggest that this is incredibly lacking in U.S. Catholic faith formation.

As this excerpt from the U.S. bishops illustrates, racism not only mocks the Golden Rule of Jesus, but denies the mystery of the incarnation, and thereby disregarding the *Imago Dei* among those who are deemed members of an inferior race. Even in the twentieth century, the U.S. Church, at least in word, upheld that fundamental to the Catholic faith is the rejection of racism in all its forms. An act of racism that "blots out the image of God" is not only idolatrous but iconoclastic. Catholics rightfully express indignation when they hear of a vandalized church or a desecrated Eucharist, but if the faithful adhered to these words from the U.S. bishops' pastoral letter, their outrage against racism would be loud, pronounced, and demand change. However, a lapse in catechesis, or more likely a lack of true grounding of the tenet of the image of God borne in every person, results in the incongruence in the Catholic response to each of these attacks.

Racism is a sin against God and humanity. This injustice divides humanity, and one who promotes racism not only places a barrier between those deemed inferior, but in denying the *Imago Dei* in the other, he or she denies the *Imago Dei* in oneself. Racism removes the one holding racist beliefs from the divine communion of the Trinity, and out of a false sense of superiority enthrones oneself in a temporal palace of sand. Racism therefore not only harms the one who is marginalized, but also harms the one who does the marginalizing.

God the Creator brings forth every person to life, regardless of race. The Creator shows no partiality—all the skin colors God created are good. Racism denies what the Giver of Life calls Good. Racism often leads people to deem some lives have less value because of race and to murder those of a specific skin color. Racism, therefore, is not pro-life, for it is against God, the Giver of Life. God hates racism. So must we.

Racism is not only a sin, but it is heretical. Merriam-Webster defines the term *heresy* as follows:

1. Adherence to a religious opinion contrary to church dogma.
2. Denial of a revealed truth by a baptized member of the Roman Catholic Church.
3. Doctrine contrary to church dogma.[4]

Thus, any belief or practice that denies, diminishes, or contradicts this important truth of the *Imago Dei* as set forth in Genesis is, by definition, heretical. Racism, a belief in the inferiority of one race and the superiority of another, denies the inherent dignity in all humans, is not only a sin as defined by the Church, but is heresy. Racism is antithetical to human dignity, the work of God, and the goodness of God.

Let that sink in: *racism is heresy*.

We often associate heresy with the denial of the humanity or divinity of Jesus, incongruent beliefs on the real presence of Christ in the Eucharist, and eternal life being dependent on our own efforts as opposed to the gratuitous mercy of God. The term *heretic* is often wielded against those who are perceived to hold positions contrary to those of the magisterium on marriage and the family. But when do we hear about racism being a heresy? From a slur to a swastika, racism in all its forms is heretical, and the Church must be vocal in naming racism as heresy.

Racism denies God's omnipotence, suggesting that God created certain humans as being inferior to others. Racism denies God's perfect love, suggesting that God created certain humans as superior to others because God loves them more.

THE CATHOLIC CHURCH AND THE STRUGGLE FOR RACIAL JUSTICE

Racism makes a liar out of God, and suggests that some of God's creation is junk. The heresy of racism is diabolical, diverting the faith from a God who loves every person regardless of race, and enabling a counterfeit Christian practice that does not challenge wrongly held beliefs on races different than one's own.

Thus, Catholics should not dismiss racial justice as "leftist." Rather, the message of Christ to love every neighbor (see Mark 12:31), coupled with the theology of the Church fathers on the *Imago Dei*, undeniably demonstrate that racial justice is an intrinsically Catholic position, orthodox in nature. Christianity and racism are incompatible, since the latter denies the place of a loving God who calls us all to love the other as oneself.

When we consider the heresy of racism, we need to hold it up against the image of the Trinity creating all of humanity—every race, skin tone, eye color, and hair color—and calling each person God's own divine handiwork. The image of God in human form cannot be contained in a single pigmentation; rather, in the divine perfection, God imprints the *Imago Dei* on a multicultural matrix, calling not only every person, but every race *good*. God sees the divine image in each of us, but the sin and the heresy of racism prevents us from seeing the *Imago Dei* in the one whose skin is different than ours. As a result, when we fail to see God in the one who has darker sin, we simply fail to see God. We also fall short in loving God and following Christ.

In the creation of humanity, God freely imparts the divine image to all persons, thereby infusing us with immense irrevocable dignity. The heresy of racism denies this dignity and leads us away from the divine communion of the Trinity, a Communion of Love who welcomes all of us into communion, bearing from our birth the divine image. How can we authentically enter the divine communion in Heaven, let alone the divine communion on Earth, if we are unwilling to accept the divine image in all persons?

In the next chapter, we will continue to reflect on the Church fathers, building upon the *Imago Dei* expressed in multicultural humanity that, by the grace of the death and resurrection of Christ, represents the multicultural, universal Body of Christ—*the Church.*

3

RACISM

The Antithesis of the Catholicity of the Church

We have read how racism is a sin against the *Imago Dei* present in all people, and that the denial of this truth is heresy. It follows that racism is contrary to the identity of the Church—the multicultural Body of Christ—and thus the universality of the Church.

The descriptive word of our faith is *Catholic* (Καθολικός), from the Greek for *universal*. Specifically, *Catholic* is a combination of two Greek words, *kata* (according to) and *holos* (whole). Racism, a sin that divides and elevates one race over another, directly conflicts with the identity of the Church as whole. Thus, racism attacks not only human dignity, but the very nature of the Body of Christ. The heretical notion of racism directly opposes the vision of the Church as worldwide and welcoming all peoples and endorses a parallel pseudo-Church that does not have Christ as its head but a counterfeit idol.

The Church fathers emphasized the universality of the Church. Reflecting on a homily on the Psalms by St. Augustine,

Racism

Henri de Lubac comments that as there were twelve tribes of Israel there are Twelve Apostles—*twelve* signifies universality.[1] Additionally, St. John Chrysostom states, "Christ makes a single body. Thus he who lives in Rome may look on the Indians as his own members."[2] St. Gregory of Nyssa writes, "The one who beholds the Church (in her universality) really beholds Christ."[3] And a quote attributed to St. Justin Martyr poignantly illustrates the incompatibility of racism with the universality of the Church:

> We used to hate and destroy one another and refused to associate with people of another race or country. Now, because of Christ, we live together with such people and pray for our enemies.

As Justin says, the encounter with Christ leads us away from animosity toward people of different races and toward conversion, which allows us to live with those we once persecuted. Members of the faith cannot be whole when believing certain races are inferior.

The Great Commission at the end of Matthew's Gospel is a new commandment from the risen Jesus to proclaim the good news to *all* people and make disciples from *every* nation (see Matt 28:19–20). Jesus calls every person regardless of skin tone as worthy of the gospel, worthy to be a child of God, and worthy to be his disciple. The early Church took this mission to heart, establishing communities not just in Greece and Rome but in Syria, Ethiopia, Egypt, and India. Without geographic expansion, the Roman Empire would have suppressed the early Church and halted Christianity's trajectory. The Church would not have been able to survive without embracing its evangelical call to be global and multicultural.

Rooted in the belief that all people bear within them the infinite gift of the *Imago Dei*, Christ calls his Church to universality. The gift of God becoming human was not limited to a certain race or peoples, but as evident in the ministry of Jesus, God's self-gift is for all peoples. Jews, Samaritans, and Romans alike experienced the healing, merciful love of Jesus, and Christ called his disciples to venture beyond Asia Minor.

The Church came forth at Pentecost by the gift of the Holy Spirit. One of the ways this gift was revealed was through the disciples speaking in new tongues and people of various nationalities simultaneously hearing the disciples speak in their own respective languages (see Acts 2:4, 6–7). Hence, the Spirit came to unite people of different lands and tongues. The Church came forth as a place for all peoples to call home (see Isa 56:7). Christianity uniquely offered a religion whose members were not solely of one ethnicity. This faith tradition revealed a God who came for all of humanity and called all people. On Pentecost, the Holy Spirit ratified the divine calling to unite peoples of different races and tongues to call one another brother and sister, children of the same Father.

However, racism drives certain people out of this home for all, and works against the Holy Spirit who unites people of different races. By the exclusion of certain peoples from the family of God, Christ himself is excluded. Racism contradicts the Great Commission and the gospel at its core. Therefore, racism is anti-Church and anti-Christ. Even the image of Heaven in the Book of Revelation describes a great multitude from every nation, tribe, and language (Rev 7:9). Therefore, racism is antithetical to the Kingdom of God. The Church must mirror the universality it was instilled with at the beginning and prophesied to reflect in Heaven according to Revelation.

On the universality of the Church, de Lubac offers this consideration: "Like sanctity, Catholicity is primarily an intrinsic feature of the Church."[4] The Church's identity is in its catholicity as is its Christ-bestowed sanctity. When we engage in tribalism and subvert the universality of the Church, as is often the case in the U.S. Church, we not only harm the catholicity of the Church, but we infringe on its holiness. Racism and tribalism makes unholy what is meant to be holy within the Church.

De Lubac notes that the early Church fathers, from Ambrose to Tertullian to Origen to Augustine, affirmed the Church as a global institution,[5] as a place where all people, created in God's image, are called into oneness. Sadly, our present-day Church is Eurocentric, and the U.S. Church is often cacophonous, neglecting and diminishing the ancient roots of the Church in Africa, the Middle East, and Asia. How many popes have been men of Italian descent, followed by men of European descent? Not since the very first popes has there been one who was brown. Our Church does not reflect universality but whiteness, even including images of a white, European Christ.

For many Catholics of color, worship spaces that exclusively use white images to portray images of our faith contribute to the white supremacist undercurrents in the Church. Images of a white Jesus promote a false idol, one that leads us further and further away from the gospel. The white Jesus results in believers who are apathetic or antipathetic to Black people and persons of color. Moreover, the depictions of a white Jesus negate the inherently multicultural nature of the Body of Christ and contradict the idea that the divine image is imprinted on all persons.

The negative reaction to a painting of the *Pietà* displayed at The Catholic University of America's law school that depicted a Black Mary and the deceased body of Jesus with a face resembling George Floyd's, coupled with the theft of this painting and death threats leveled against the artist,[6] signify the amount of resistance in the Church to its call to universality. Imaging a Jesus who is not white, especially one that bears an image of one who signaled the need for racial justice in society and especially in the Church, triggered vociferous animosity from those who, whether they realize it or not, serve the idol of whiteness as opposed to Christ. This revealed how far the Church has strayed from its root call of catholicity.

Even the pontificate of Francis, the first pope from Latin America, encountered backlash from pockets holding onto a Eurocentric basis for the Church. Even though he is of Italian descent, Pope Francis offers the Church a unique perspective as a child of immigrants who grew up on a continent other than Europe and engaged with a different mix of people. One cannot separate his pastoral approach for the divorced and civilly remarried expressed in *Amoris laetitia* from his experience of the Church in Latin America, where the growing divorced populace feels excluded from the sacraments and thus from the Church herself.

Four cardinals submitted five *dubia* related to this apostolic exhortation, including the pastoral approach to the divorced. These cardinals lead an opposition within the Church that continues to be an area of tension. They claim that what Pope Francis teaches in *Amoris laetitia* regarding the divorced and civilly remarried is a break from the Church's moral teachings.[7]

A pastoral application requires a global perspective, however. This is what I believe is lacking in those who oppose the greater nuance Francis promotes in *Amoris laetitia*. Much of the counterargument is an appeal to tradition and assumes that Pope Francis is breaking from it. However, if the objection is "we've always done it this way," then the larger and more significant break from tradition is the devolution of the Church from a global, multicultural, universal basis to a Eurocentric Church. This must first be remedied, and only then can the opposing cardinals and their adherents appreciate the pastoral approach Francis advocates for.

Pope Francis also expresses a global concern in his encyclical *Laudato si'* and in his post-synodal exhortation *Querida Amazonia*. In *Laudato si'*, Francis emphasizes the injustice toward the underdeveloped world, whereby economic interests usurp an area's resources at the expense of the people who live there. Appealing to the theme of viewing the Earth as "our common home," Francis reminds the Church that our concern is for all of humanity. "The urgent challenge to protect our common home includes a concern to bring the whole human family together to seek a sustainable and integral development.... Humanity still has the ability to work together in building our common home" (13).

While there are those in the Church who have repudiated *Laudato si'* as leftist propaganda, and many U.S. bishops have remained silent on this encyclical,[8] Pope Francis attempts to realign the Church to its global origin. I believe much of the resistance points to a deeper reaction to this shift in influence. Although Christ tasked the Church at its inception with a global mission, human influence centered the axis around Europe, and there are those in the Church who are fighting against the return to a global vision.

This is further exemplified in *Querida Amazonia*. The exhortation focuses on the struggles of the Indigenous people in the Amazon and the Church's obligation to accompany them. Continuing the theme from *Laudato si'*, Francis deplores the colonizing interests (9) along with the destruction of the natural surroundings due to the imbalance of power (13). The twofold redirection of the Church to (1) a global mission and (2) the marginalized directly opposes a Eurocentric Church that upholds whiteness and exploitation.

The main criticism of this exhortation from critics of Pope Francis was directed to his call for "a necessary process of inculturation that rejects nothing of the goodness that already exists in Amazonian cultures, but brings it to fulfilment in the light of the Gospel" (66). This repudiation was underlined by the reaction to the presence at the synod of carved images displaying a naked pregnant woman, resembling the Amazonian indigenous symbol of "Pachamama." Critics decried this display as idolatry and syncretism, leading even an Austrian Catholic, Alexander Tschugguel, to throw what he labeled "Pachamama idols" into the Tiber.[9] On hearing of it, Pope Francis apologized for this destructive and harmful act.[10] As Francis already stated in the apostolic exhortation, "It is possible to take up an indigenous symbol in some way, without necessarily considering it as idolatry. A myth charged with spiritual meaning can be used to advantage and not always considered a pagan error" (79).

Francis's pontificate marks a global shift, an attempt to return the Church to the roots of its catholicity. I am grateful to live in an era of this pontificate, as Francis strives to repair the breach within the Church so that it can fulfill its global, multicultural identity. However, the backlash to Francis's efforts further emphasizes how far the Church is from Christ's inherent call to catholicity. The Church has strayed from its identity: a Church that promotes whiteness is a Church that is not Catholic, and by being less Catholic, we have become less holy. To move forward, the Church must work to become Catholic again and must start by naming and denouncing its favoritism toward whiteness and Eurocentricity. This includes the Church's complicity with colonization[11] and slavery.[12]

Here are two instances of Eurocentric condescension that had a negative impact on Indian Catholics.

Latinization of the Syro-Malabar Rite and the Schism among the St. Thomas Christians

Many Catholics from Kerala, India, where my parents are from, are members of the Syro-Malabar Rite. This is one of the Eastern Catholic Churches that claims lineage from the evangelization of St. Thomas the Apostle. Thomas established the East Syrian Church, and following the trade routes of that time, continued his evangelization into India in 52 CE. The St. Thomas Christians are therefore descended from the earliest Christians—a truth that is rarely celebrated.

However, twelve centuries later, the Portuguese arrived in southern India, and their clergy determined that the faith practices of the St. Thomas Christians were not in line with the Catholic Church. This is astounding given that Christianity had been practiced in Kerala long before it had been in Portugal, but this is the fruit of Eurocentrism and racism, robbing a people of its inherent goodness, dignity, and value. Racism caused the Portuguese clergy to miss how wrong they were to subjugate the Indian Christians who received their faith directly from the one who placed his hands in the wounds of Christ (see John 20:27).

In 1599, the Latin Rite archbishop of Goa, Alexis de Menezes, convoked the Synod of Diamper. The six-day synod aimed to Latinize the liturgy of the St. Thomas Christians and to correct "errors." For instance, the synod falsely accused the St. Thomas Christians of Nestorianism, an ancient heresy that denied the unity of the human and divine natures in Christ. In protest, many of the Indian clergy refused to attend the synod. Because adherence to the synod was under the threat of excommunication, an estimated half of the St. Thomas Christians left the Church, opposing this Latin imposition at an event known as the Coonan Cross Oath. These Indian Christians swore they would not submit to Rome, and instead they aligned themselves with the Orthodox Patriarch of Antioch.

The racism of the Portuguese clergy divided the Body of Christ and resulted in many Indian Christians leaving the Catholic Church. While the Portuguese clergy accused the St. Thomas Christians of heresy, it was their own racism that led them to heresy against this ancient Christian community, resulting in the corruption of its ancient liturgy and schism within the Church in Kerala.

One of the ways that Latinization permanently changed the Syro-Malabar Church was the imposition of mandatory celibacy for the priests of the rite. Prior to the Synod of Diamper, Syro-Malabar priests, like their other Eastern Catholic counterparts, were permitted to be married, with bishops selected from among the celibate priests. To date, the Syro-Malabar Church has made no plan to reinstitute married clergy, though it would be canonically valid.

The effect of this was the alteration of the original identity of the Syro-Malabar Church. Today's Syro-Malabar Rite is a shadow of its former self. A Church that is universal at its core respects the differences in various cultures and rites and seeks not to impose but to appreciate the God-given uniqueness of how the Body of Christ is made visible through other cultures, languages, and rites.

The Destructive Bias of Francis Xavier

Around the same time as the Portuguese infiltration in India, Jesuit missionary St. Francis Xavier spent eight months in Goa. He was instrumental in the mass proselytization of the Goans, whose land had been usurped as a Portuguese colony.[13]

Since grade school, I had considered Francis Xavier one of my favorite saints, especially since my family is from India. Stories of his apostolic zeal, the countless people he baptized, and his desire to spread the gospel throughout Asia bolstered my faith. Before entering the Jesuits, I visited his church in Goa in the summer of 2009, and had an exclusive viewing of his relics. During the thirty-day Spiritual Exercises retreat while I was a Jesuit novice, I read *The Letters and Instructions of Francis Xavier*, but I read that he said Indians made for poor vocations due to their lack of commitment both to the order and to celibacy. I took the saint's words at face value. How could a saint be wrong?

Internalizing these words led me to believe that there was something intrinsically wrong with me as an Indian that made me incapable and unfit to serve as a priest. Because this was difficult to accept, I then decided that I was different than the Indians Xavier was referring to since I was Westernized, having been born and raised in the United States, and had a lineage that included the early Jewish Christians. I was not like the Hindu converts or the impoverished fisherman that Xavier made such comments about.

As I now sit with Xavier's words and my reactions to them, I realize that the saint was wrong in his harmful, negative view of the Indian people, and that I was wrong in internalizing this negative view and applying that to my fellow Indians.

Further in Xavier's writings, he often referred to the Indians as "Negroes"[14] and viewed the people he was missioned to serve with disdain, influenced by the Portuguese colonists. Today, Xavier's reference to the color of the Goans' skin is not only cringe-inducing, but truly shameful:

> [Indians] being black themselves, consider their own color the best, they believe that their gods are black… the great majority of their idols are as black as black can be…and seem to be as dirty as they are ugly and horrible to look at.[15]

Even more deplorable, Francis Xavier himself asked for a Court of Inquisition in Goa. The Goan inquisition, described by Marathi historian and activist A. K. Priolkar as a "terrible tribunal" of torture,[16] resulted in the brutalization and deaths of countless native Goans. One source deemed the Goan inquisition a "holocaust,"[17] particularly since there were Jews in Goa who had escaped the Inquisition in Europe only to be persecuted in India.

The Inquisition rendered the practice of Hinduism and Islam, along with the use of the local language Konkani, punishable by death. The Portuguese colonists even took Hindu children from their families. In addition, they burned villages, raped and seized women as slaves, and tortured native Goans with public floggings, burning them at the stake, and tying them to torture wheels.[18] Death and defilement were committed in the name of Christ, but by doing this, Xavier and the Portuguese colonists crucified the *Imago Dei* of the Goan people.

One would have hoped that Xavier would have regarded the Indians as Christ would, particularly given the Jesuit call to find God in all things. Xavier fell short in recognizing the *Imago Dei* in the Indian people. Additionally, he fell short of the words of his order's founder, Ignatius of Loyola, who instructed Jesuits sent on mission to "look upon" those they had been entrusted with "as someone bathed in the blood of Christ, an image of God, a temple of the Holy Spirit."[19]

Despite the saint's harmful words and actions, the people of Goa celebrate Francis Xavier as a hero. Like many nonwhite people, they were deluded into venerating whiteness and disowning their own God-given skin. While many were baptized at the famous hand of Xavier, the saint missed the opportunity of experiencing his own deepening conversion by recognizing the presence of God in the Indian people.

Let us reflect on what the Church needs to exhibit to be truly *catholic*:

> A truly *catholic* Church would reflect the Spirit that breathed the Church into life, one that was not

exclusive but accessible to a plurality of races and languages since the beginning.

A truly *catholic* Church would uphold the dignity of all people.

A truly *catholic* Church would have representations of Jesus that are truly catholic.

A truly *catholic* Church would respect the expression of the faith as exhibited by a cultural context, and like God, delight in it and call it good (see Gen 1:31).

A truly *catholic* Church would not be Eurocentric but one that every person could call home.

In truth, the Church's multicultural people and expressions enrich the faith and more closely resemble the expansive and all-encompassing Trinity, who created all peoples in its image and deemed them good. As Pope Francis exhorts in *Evangelii gaudium*, "We would not do justice to the logic of the incarnation if we thought of Christianity as monocultural and monotonous" (117).

God became human and died for all peoples. Christ sought to have all peoples receive his Word. The Body of Christ therefore is not solely to be depicted as European but as Japanese, Black, Sri Lankan, Cambodian, and Guarani. Christ bears the image of the outcast, whether that be the migrant or refugee, the Romani begging for food and money, or the malnourished hopelessly lying on the roads.

We cannot let racism attack the Church from within and destroy its identity. Racism infringes on the four marks of the Church: one, holy, catholic, and apostolic.

Racism denies that we are all one, created in the image of God.

Racism denies the *Imago Dei* in all people regardless of race, and thereby defiles in another what God made holy.

Racism denies the catholicity of the Church by promoting that some races are better than other races, thereby discrediting the multicultural framework of the Church.

Racism denies the apostolic mission from Christ to proclaim the gospel to all peoples.

Hence, the sin and heresy of racism disintegrates the God-given identity of the Church. We, through the grace of our baptism, must work toward promoting the catholicity of the Church by working against the sin and heresy of racism within it.

Parts 2 and 3 of this book delve into the lived experience of the sin and heresy of racism in the Church in recent times. We will step into the abyss of how the sin of racism has divided the Church, especially in the United States, and despite efforts to direct the U.S. Church to take an active stand against racism, these words have not been put to practice and nonwhite Catholics, the fastest growing demographic in the American Church, continue to be disenfranchised by their own Catholic family. The cure is conversion, which by the grace of God we must seek to root out that which holds us back from loving all people, and in turn permit our Church to heal and become the united Body Christ intended it to be.

RACISM AND A DIVIDED CHURCH

4

A HOUSE OF DIVIDED BISHOPS CANNOT STAND AGAINST RACISM

> Racism is a virus that quickly mutates and, instead of disappearing, goes into hiding and lurks in waiting. Instances of racism continue to shame us, for they show that our supposed social progress is not as real or definitive as we think.[1]
>
> —Pope Francis

The year 2020 awakened me to the heightened degree of division in the U.S. Catholic Church.

I grew up in a Church very aware of the conservative/liberal labels used by both clergy and laity. My upbringing was in a conservative camp, while my education and Jesuit formation gave me exposure to more liberal influences in the Church. However, as a person of Indian origin, I never realized racism was an area of disagreement among Catholics. Surely Nazism and white supremacy are intrinsically evil. Surely the examples of Dr. Martin Luther King Jr. and Rosa Parks exhibit the gospel. Surely Catholics at their core are against racism in all its forms. The year 2020 proved that wrong.

My ignorance was my own fault. I was unaware of how pervasive racism is, not just in the society and in the Church, but in my own life. Coming from an immigrant family, I assumed that my place in society was that of an outsider. To feel like I didn't belong was the norm, not the exception. When the norm is inferiority, it is difficult to realize how damaging and unjust it is.

Thus, I became subservient to the norm. As an Indian American, I fell into the mold of American society's expectation of my people—the "model minority." Asian Americans, inclusive of South Asian Americans, grew up with the expectation that we would fall in line with American society: pay taxes, obey laws, work hard, keep our heads downs, and align ourselves with American beliefs and values, which often translates as *white* American beliefs and values. As such, recognizing and challenging racism in both society and the Church in the United States are taboo.

My experiences in Nogales, Mexico, and in Honduras penetrated my former stereotypes of those seeking to come to the United States over the southern border. I did not realize that the rhetoric against migrants from Mexico and Central and South America was built on a racist premise that "these people" do not belong in "our" country. This rhetoric causes an other-ing of our neighbors from these countries as being less-than, too low to be worthy to enter the United States. However, many Catholics espouse this belief and name such people "illegals." Pew Research reported that 81 percent of Catholic Republicans favor expanding the wall along the U.S.-Mexico border.[2] This is appalling given how clear the Church's stance is on migrants and refugees, regardless of whether they are legal or undocumented.

In the USCCB's pastoral letter *Welcoming the Stranger among Us: Unity in Diversity* (2000), the U.S. bishops uphold that an immigrant, regardless of legal status, is made in the *Imago Dei* and is deserving of commensurate dignity:

> Without condoning undocumented migration, the Church supports the human rights of all people and offers them pastoral care, education, and social services, no matter what the circumstances of entry into this country, and it works for the respect of the human dignity of all—especially those who find themselves in desperate circumstances. We recognize that nations have the right to control their borders. We also recognize and strongly assert that all human persons, created as they are in the image of God, possess a fundamental dignity that gives rise to a more compelling claim to the conditions worthy of human life.

The bishops assert that the *Imago Dei* is the more compelling claim. But why is this message unheard by so many U.S. Catholics? For the same reason so many Catholics saw no wrong in the murder of an unarmed Black man by a white police officer in Minneapolis on May 25, 2020. Many of these are the same people who decry the Black Lives Matter movement as Marxist, against Church teaching, and promoting hatred and violence. This is the same crowd that responds to Black Lives Matter with "All Lives Matter," "Blue Lives Matter," and "Back the Badge."

The straightforward messages from the gospel, Church teaching, the Church fathers, several popes, and even the USCCB on human dignity, the *Imago Dei*, and the sin of racism become clouded in the lived experiences of Catholics when personal biases and convictions go unexamined. This results in a hardness of heart that prevents the truth of Christ from penetrating it and bearing fruit. The Holy Spirit reveals our blind spots, some of which are unconscious biases and idols that compete with the

Lord, and convicts us of our disintegration with the God who created all people equally and loves every person.

The larger problem is that some members of the U.S. hierarchy also subscribe to these biased convictions over the teachings of Christ. Additionally, there are bishops, regardless of their personal beliefs, who are not willing to challenge them. This weakness in the U.S. hierarchy placates these people rather than challenging their harmful convictions. This would be a truly pastoral challenge, for not only do these Catholics injure others with these un-Christian positions, but they also further alienate themselves from God and neighbor by espousing that which is in direct conflict to the gospel call.

Let us examine this house of divided bishops through the lens of the Trinity. The divided episcopal house goes against the catholicity of the Church, particularly the call to wholeness. This is particularly true when the subject is racism—a sin that divides and promotes an imbalance within humanity. I pray that the Spirit bring true conviction to all members of our Church, especially those charged with leading and shepherding it.

Examining the Divided Episcopal House

The scribes who had come from Jerusalem said, "[Jesus] is possessed by Beelzebul," and "By the prince of demons he drives out demons."

Summoning them, [Jesus] began to speak to them in parables, "How can Satan drive out Satan? If a kingdom is divided against itself, that kingdom cannot stand. And if a house is divided against itself, that house will not be able to stand. And if Satan has risen up against himself and is divided, he cannot

A House of Divided Bishops Cannot Stand against Racism

stand; that is the end of him. But no one can enter a strong man's house to plunder his property unless he first ties up the strong man. Then he can plunder his house. (Mark 3:22–27)

Division in the Church is usually the work of the evil spirit. It thwarts the Church's promotion of the mission of Christ, who offered his life for all of humanity. On the issue of racism, an unambiguous evil for any follower of Christ, the fact that those who are called to be shepherds cannot denounce it suggests that great harm is being done that is subtle yet destructive, promoting both sin and division in the Body of Christ.

While I do not believe any bishop, in his heart of hearts, desires to support anything contrary to the gospel of Jesus, if we are not attentive to discernment of spirits, any one of us can be led astray unawares. The Church's shepherds are most vulnerable to this because they have such an impact on the spiritual health and faith formation of those they are called to serve. Given the role of a bishop in forming and leading those in his care—clergy, religious, and laity—it is of utmost importance that they model for the faithful a complete and unambiguous rejection of racism in all its forms.

Examining this divided episcopal house is like viewing a home after a fire or natural disaster. There is tremendous loss and sadness along with discouragement, but the Spirit offers us the virtue of courage. A destroyed home can be rebuilt. This requires dedication and patience, but by the grace of God, we too, laity and clergy alike, can join in the call of Francis of Assisi and rebuild the divided episcopal house.

First, however, we must examine the damage before we can rebuild.

For most of my entire life as a cradle Catholic, I had no issues with the USCCB. I assumed the bishops did God's work, and anyone who had a problem with them likely had their own issues with the Church's teaching. However, the murder of George Floyd opened my eyes to the sad division among the U.S. bishops. Several prelates that I had looked up to as a young adult Catholic let the Church and me down by their inability to denounce emphatically and unequivocally the murder of George Floyd and the anti-Black racism at the root of this crime.

As with the sad realization that our elders are not always models in certain respects, this experience caused me to grow up quickly and respond to God's prophetic call. This does not justify the weakness among several of the U.S. bishops nor their lackluster response to the sin of racism occurring before their very eyes. Some of the troubling messages from U.S. bishops include the following:

- Following the outcry against police brutality and the need for greater accountability among law enforcement, Cardinal Timothy Dolan penned a tone-deaf article that appeared in the *New York Post* titled "For God's Sake, Stop Demonizing the NYPD"[3] that made a minimal response to George Floyd and was centrally ordered to defend and support the police. Dolan also decried the removal of remnants of hate such as Confederate monuments and statues as "dangerous."[4]
- Following the murder of George Floyd, Bishop Robert Barron published an article on his *Word on Fire* site titled "Why 'What Are the Bishops Doing About It' Is the Wrong Question,"[5] stating that the work of racial justice is the laity's job.
- Archbishop Jose Gómez characterizes social justice movements as "pseudo-religions, and even replacements and rivals to traditional Christian beliefs."[6]

A House of Divided Bishops Cannot Stand against Racism

When prominent, vocal bishops take a stand against the racially oppressed, they appear to speak for the Church and manifest that it is turning its back on Black people and persons of color. This is particularly disturbing when prelates take issue with an organization that advocates for the dignity of Black lives. In the next section, we will examine the negative responses to the Black Lives Matter movement (BLM), reasons for the animosity, and the need for the U.S. Church to offer a united front against American society's persistent diminishment of the value of Black lives.

Episcopal Animosity toward *Black Lives Matter*

Following the killing of George Floyd, the president and CEO of Catholic Charities of Eastern Washington, Dr. Rob McCann, expressed in a video address the need for an authentic voice amid racial injustice in the United States:

> Watching what has unfolded and listening to the voices of the marginalized since the death of George Floyd has changed me in a way that is likely long overdue....I am a racist....How could I not be? As a white person living in America where every institution is geared to advantage people who look like me, it's seemingly impossible to be anything other than a racist....The bias of white people supports and feeds into powerfully racist systems in our country. As a Catholic who believes in reconciliation, I must own my part in that and treat it like any other sin.[7]

Additionally, McCann acknowledged that the Catholic Church and Catholic Charities are racist and must fight against racism, including but not limited to the Church's role in and silence on slavery, and the harm to Indigenous people in Church-run residential schools. Furthermore, McCann pointed out the inequity in having a Catholic Charities board, leadership team, and staff mostly comprised of white people, even though its mission is to serve people who are disproportionately nonwhite. The organization must own and make amends for this.

In response to the video, Bishop Thomas Daly of Spokane took issue with McCann's message, labeling it as divisive and for being interpreted as "levying false accusations against 'whites' and the Catholic Church." Rather than consider McCann's personal and candid reflection on the role of white privilege and racism, Daly's response was emblematic of white fragility as described by Dr. Robin DiAngelo.[8] When confronted with the beneficial status that white people have in society and their complicity in it, white fragility causes defensive and combative reactions. Daly's message moves from white fragility to an attack on the Black Lives Matter movement:

> [McCann's] support of the Black Lives Matter organization (BLM), albeit now modified, puzzles me. BLM is in conflict with Church teaching regarding marriage, family and the sanctity of life....One need not stand with BLM to stand for Black lives.[9]

Here, Bishop Daly creates a false dichotomy between BLM and the Catholic Church, a rhetoric that reverberates in Catholic circles and discourages Catholic involvement in a movement that promotes the dignity of Black lives. While Daly might be correct that part of the BLM organization espouses an ideology that is pro-LGBTQ and pro-choice, I would ask the bishop and anyone who supports his logic to reflect on the following:

- Are Catholics involved in the Republican Party? Are *all* Republican platforms in concert with Church teaching?
- Are Catholics involved in the pro-life movement? Do Catholics in the pro-life movement agree with *all* the positions held by non-Catholics in the pro-life movement?

Then why cannot Catholics collaborate with BLM on the shared interest of the dignity of Black lives? As will be expressed in part 3, there is much gaslighting employed to divert Catholics away from seeing the importance of the dignity of Black lives.

There is a distinction between the Black Lives Matter Global Network and the BLM movement. The former espouses the areas Daly alluded to, whereas the latter includes people who are focused on racial justice and might not agree with all the tenets of the BLM Global Network. Moreover, while Daly is correct that, in theory, one need not be in BLM to stand for Black lives, in practice there has been little involvement of Catholics in anti-Black racial justice outside of movements such as BLM. Catholics would not have heard of Trayvon Martin, Tamir Rice, Ahmaud Arbery, Breonna Taylor, or George Floyd had it not been for the efforts of BLM.

Daly is not the only bishop who publicly opposed BLM. While not as vocal as Daly, Archbishop Alexander Sample of Portland warned Catholics against "aligning themselves with 'simple catchphrases' and 'movements,'" saying that "we need to speak from our own tradition on race."[10] This continues the theme of falsely dichotomizing BLM and the Catholic faith rather than employing a both/and approach. Additionally, we as Catholics cannot credibly "'speak from our own tradition' on race" without reflecting on and repenting of our Church's role in racial injustice. If our Church does not directly and organically state that Black Lives Matter, then we need to learn how to better work for the dignity of Black lives from those who do make this statement.

Thus, the U.S. bishops have much work to do to counteract the prevalence of racism in the Church and in society. With a membership that is 88 percent white,[11] the members of the USCCB need to own and work through their privilege, individually and collectively, to minister to *all* God's people with whom they have been entrusted more effectively. When this privilege is actively dealt with, Barron and his brother bishops might better traverse this so-called abyss with the gifts of humility and compassion.

Why are some U.S. bishops so entrenched in their opposition to BLM? The reason is less divine and more worldly, namely, the power of *money*. While there is a browning effect[12] in the U.S. Church, most donations come from a wealthy white minority, like the donor base for *Word on Fire*.

Aidan McAleenan, pastor of a Black Catholic parish in Oakland, alluded to this same dynamic. "The bishops are more worried about white sensibility and the white European church, and they don't want to hurt their people. I think it's about this, if you're going to be really honest about it, money, at the end of the day."[13] Money talks, and bishops listen. McAleenan further commented on the U.S. bishops and the death of George Floyd: "The bishops of the United States have their knee on the neck of the people of God, the church. We need as a church to be able to breathe."[14]

Fr. McAleenan sums up well how disgruntled many Catholics feel when they see the bishops' ambiguous, divided, and lukewarm response to racial injustice. Rather than joining in peaceful protests, some bishops would prefer to tear apart a movement that is filling the void left by the U.S. Church's own lack of outreach to Black and Brown communities. Rather than protest the murder of an unarmed Black man, some bishops would prefer to justify the knee to his neck and pat the offending officers on the back for a job well done.

While some bishops believe the current social justice movements differ from the Civil Rights Movement of the 1960s, I suggest that these same bishops would have been too cowardly to march with Dr. King and would continue to appease their white congregants and donors. These same bishops would have labeled King a Marxist as they do BLM and social justice movements to obfuscate the work being done to promote human dignity. The U.S. Church will not be fruitful if it continues this trajectory of a tepid and impractical response to the evil of racism.

What about all those pastoral letters the U.S. bishops have written on racism? Do they not demonstrate that the bishops have taken a stand against racial injustice? And if so, why do prominent bishops seem to believe the opposite? We will explore these themes in the next chapter, but until the U.S. bishops can unanimously state that Black Lives Matter and put these words into actions, any forthcoming pastoral letter on racism is just words on a page.

5

EMPTY WORDS AND EMPTY PROMISES

Although we saw in part 1 that the sin and heresy of racism can be found in the beginning of the Scriptures and among the early Church fathers, it is shocking that, according to Catholic speaker Gloria Purvis, the U.S. bishops denounced racial prejudice as immoral *for the first time* as late as 1958.[1] The U.S. Church was a coconspirator and beneficiary of racism and white supremacy, supporting segregation and even preventing seminaries[2] and convents[3] from accepting Black people.

Eventually, in the twentieth century the USCCB began issuing multiple pastoral letters on racism, but what really was needed was a *mea culpa* for the Church's role in U.S. racism and an active plan to make amends, but it is easier to talk about the sin that is coming from the outside rather than what is inside. The series of pastoral letters, culminating in 2018, are nice words with some nice ideals, but as we will see in the forthcoming pages, there is little change in the U.S. Church's practices toward Black and Brown communities because there is no authentic call for conversion within the Church for its complicity in racism, particularly among its leaders. The U.S. Church needs an overhaul in responding to the sin of racism, but thus far has proven deaf to this call from God.

Discrimination and the Christian Conscience (1958)

Ms. Purvis alluded to the U.S. bishops' pastoral letter *Discrimination and the Christian Conscience*. This was released four years after the historic Supreme Court decision *Brown v. Topeka Board of Education*, which ruled that segregation in public schools is unconstitutional.

While a product of its time (for example, Black people are referred to as "Negroes" or "colored"), this letter offers several important challenges to the divide on racism in the United States:

- The letter reiterates a statement from the U.S. bishops issued in 1943 that calls for "the extension of full freedom within the confines of our beloved country" to the Black community (1), along with "a special obligation of justice" (2) that includes political, economic, and educational equality, fairness in social welfare, good housing, and an unfettered opportunity for social advancement.
- The bishops call on white people "to see that our colored citizens obtain their full rights as given to them by God" (5).
- The pastoral upholds the exhortation to recognize God's universal love for all and to love one's neighbor (7), as well as the universality of the Christian faith (8).

- As referenced by Ms. Purvis, the U.S. bishops state that discrimination based on race "cannot be reconciled with the truth that God created all" people with equal rights and dignity (11).
- The letter posits that legal segregation renders inferior those who are the objects of segregation, and that segregation cannot be reconciled with the Christian faith (15). The U.S. bishops also acknowledged the oppression of the Black community caused by segregation, namely, the denial of their basic human rights (16).
- The bishops recognize the inequitable premise cited to support segregation, namely, that Black, Brown, and Indigenous people are so different from white people that they must have separate institutions, along with the hypocrisy in the acceptance and assimilation of descendants of immigrants from European nations (17).

However, there are multiple areas where the well-intentioned letter missed the mark:

- While the U.S. bishops appropriately denounce slavery and segregation, they fail to name and repent of the Church's involvement with both these evils. Both instances of structural racism are dealt with in generalities and as outside the Church rather than deeply embedded in the institution.
- While the pastoral calls on white people to "to see that our colored citizens obtain their full rights as given to them by God" (5), the actual wording in the letter begins with "we hope the overwhelming majority of our white citizens" followed by

Empty Words and Empty Promises

the referenced quote. But why do the U.S. bishops use the word *hope* and not *demand*? Why only the "overwhelming majority" of white people as opposed to *all* white people? The bishops had the opportunity to state that not only is Christianity incompatible with racism and segregation, but to support racism and segregation is incompatible with being a *Christian*. The bishops are too sensitive to the white members of the Church and not sensitive enough to the racially marginalized.

- While the pastoral letter names the universality of the Christian faith and God's love for all people, the bishops should have used stronger language, in the spirit of St. John Chrysostom, to call on white Catholics to look upon Black and Brown people with a spirit of unity and equality.
- While the U.S. bishops recognize the disparity between white assimilation and equal rights for Black, Brown, and Indigenous people, the letter observes it as a phenomenon rather than calling it out as the injustice that it is. The placating and appeasing of the white community renders the letter ineffective to produce real change.
- While the bishops "urge that concrete plans" be made to address racism (20), no such plans are given in the letter or following its release. There were several platitudes but no action steps. Subsequent pastoral letters echoed these platitudes while requiring no action.

Discrimination and the Christian Conscience attempts to offer unified pastoral guidance on racism in the United States. However, without naming the responsibility of the Church and the role of white supremacy, and rallying people toward racial justice, the document is empty and not exhortative. The appeal of social justice movements, on the other hand, is that these *actually* mobilize people into direct and immediate action to bring real assistance and support to the affected communities.

Talk is cheap, and in movements people act while their hearts are being moved. This is why the U.S. Church is foolish in denouncing, distancing itself from, and falsely dichotomizing social movements, when it should be taking notes, learning, and collaborating with them. Secular social justice movements have done more to promote the *Imago Dei* among the racially marginalized than has the Catholic Church. The Church has benefitted from and promoted racial injustice and was a bystander in its midst.

The National Race Crisis (1968)

Ten years after *Discrimination and the Christian Conscience*, the U.S. bishops said they had not done enough had "failed to do enough to change the attitudes of many believers" (4). Following *Discrimination and the Christian Conscience*, the problem of racism in America did not improve or dwindle, as likely hoped by the bishops in 1958. Instead, the year prior to *The National Race Crisis* witnessed the "long, hot summer" of racial violence, and the Reverend Dr. King was assassinated the year of the pastoral's release.

The National Race Crisis made bold steps relative to the prior pastoral on racism, including naming Catholics as among those responsible for allowing racism to persist, as well as calling out a "white segregationalist mentality" as largely responsible for the crisis (6). A call for accountability among members of the faith and classifying white supremacy was needed for the U.S. Church to promote real change in the nation in racial inequality.

Second, the bishops not only name personal racism but also institutional racism and express their desire to "commit our full energies to the task of eradicating the effects of such racism on American society" (8) and thereby promote the *Imago Dei* in all people. These steps were necessary to ensure the bishops could credibly witness to the gospel. The previous letter largely placated white Catholics. Because it did not say that Catholics were complicit with those promoting white superiority as evidenced not only in personal bias but structural racism, the problem of racial injustice would only grow in the years between the issuance of the two pastoral letters.

Third, the U.S. bishops call for an eradication of discrimination in all the works of the Church, including but not limited to parishes, schools, hospitals, nursing homes, and hospice facilities (10). The exhortation to look within and put into practice the principle that discrimination is incompatible with the Christian faith is a step that cannot be ignored. Additionally, the bishops express the need to direct resources and assistance to those who are in need. They call for an urban task force "to coordinate all Catholic activities and to relate them to those of others working for the common goal of society, based on truth, justice, and love" (13).

In a marvelously forward-thinking statement, one that the present-day bishops ought to learn from, the pastoral letter encourages Catholics to work with and ally themselves to civic groups (17–18), especially those with deep roots in the Black community. Based on this statement, one might wonder if the bishops of 1968 would be more willing to dialogue with the BLM movement than the present-day USCCB.

The letter then discusses important focus areas to ensure equality for Black Americans: education, economic opportunity, housing, and government assistance. The bishops point to education both as a basic human need and a potential remedy to the cycle of poverty and call on Catholic school systems to redouble their efforts (22). Regarding job opportunities, the bishops identify employment as a means to insure self-respect and stable family life. They call on both private and public sectors to develop programs to aid in the employment of Black people and persons of color (23).

The bishops recognize the need both for affordable housing and the removal of the barriers of segregation to suburban living (24). While the bishops do not use the terms *sundown towns*, which prohibit the presence of Black people after sundown (and thereby prevent residence as well),[4] and *redlining*, which mapped out which neighborhoods would have predominantly Black populations and thus be riskier investments,[5] as well as racial discrimination in access to housing and home financing, the bishops called for the end of these harmful practices. The bishops also acknowledge that housing segregation can be an added barrier to employment as jobs migrated from cities into suburbs. Finally, the bishops address the need for welfare programs that promote the dignity and integrity of families and call on private and public sectors to invest in this cause. "Surely the richest nation in the world can afford a massive war on poverty" (25).

In summary, *The National Race Crisis* is an improvement over what came before in owning that the last letter was insufficient, calling on Catholics to recognize their complicity in racism and on Church works to eradicate discrimination and direct themselves toward the needs of the racially marginalized, name as harmful the "white segregationist mentality," classify racism not solely as personal but structural, and offer concrete action plans and areas of focus. But did this letter curb the practice of racism within and outside the U.S. Church?

The major blow to the credibility of the pastoral came when the bishops allocated $28,000 for the Urban Task Force, high six figures for a study on the problems in the priesthood, and $2.2 million in added funds for The Catholic University of America.[6] If the poor and the racially marginalized were truly seen as having immense dignity and worthy of equality, then why was such a paltry sum designated for this important, gospel-centered work? More money should have been allocated to the Urban Task Force. When we prioritize the poor and the marginalized, we are being true and faithful to Christ.

The inconsistency between the pastoral and the designation of funds for the Urban Task Force shows how the Church's attention draws away from the gospel mission. The poor and Black and Brown communities did not benefit from the funds directed to The Catholic University. The lack of investment in these communities has increased the divide between poor and rich, nonwhite and white. Thus, words on a page, even when they seem promising, do little to promote racial justice if they are not converted into action.

Brothers and Sisters to Us (1979)

More than a decade after the promising yet faltering pastoral *The National Race Crisis*, the U.S. bishops issued *Brothers and Sisters to Us*. But before delving into the letter, we must address its problematic title. As Bryan Massingale asks, "Who's the 'us'?"[7]

When it comes to race, the bishops revealed their blind spot with this tone-deaf wording. They seem to be speaking to a white audience as if the Catholic Church in the United States is primarily made up of whites, other-ing Black Catholics and the overall Black community. This contradicts the ideal of the call to universality in the Church expressed in the prior two letters. As Mary T. Yelenick reflected, the "curious title itself reflected the racial chasm existing between Black Catholics and their counterparts."[8] The faulty wording diminishes the effectiveness of the letter and the bishops' credibility regarding racial justice. Massingale offers a further response:

THE CATHOLIC CHURCH AND THE STRUGGLE FOR RACIAL JUSTICE

The Catholic racial justice tradition tends to speak *about* and *for* aggrieved African Americans; but it does not support or acknowledge black agency, meaning independent thought, action, and leadership. There is no indication that African Americans themselves have a contribution to make toward either understanding or changing the climate of racial injustice. The American Catholic approach has been far more willing to prompt whites to concede rights to blacks than to encourage blacks to press for social justice. This cannot but render Catholic ethical reflection on racial matters inadequate and impoverished, if not even erroneous.[9]

Speaking "*about* and *for* aggrieved African Americans" is an example of the U.S. Church's paternalism and condescension toward the Black community. Rather than speak of them and to them as equals, they speak *about* and *for* them, which further shows the attitude of the U.S. bishops, who are mostly white men. The very title of this pastoral implicitly promotes white supremacy.

Having addressed the problem with the letter's title, let us turn our attention to its content. *Brothers and Sisters to Us* begins in a promising direction, stating that racism "is an evil which endures in our society and in our Church." The *and in our Church* admission is significant, as is the fact that racism is not being discussed as a bygone problem but a persistent one. However, U.S. bishops "are convinced that the majority of Americans realize that racial discrimination is both unjust and unworthy of this nation." If that were the case, then the problem of racism would not still endure in society and in the Church, and there would be no need for another pastoral to address it. The bishops completely missed the mark on this one. We can simply look to the present and note the statistic that 81 percent

Empty Words and Empty Promises

of Catholic Republicans favor expanding the wall along the U.S.-Mexico border,[10] and that is just one area of racial discrimination. The bishops' problematic stance reflects continued white appeasement as opposed to directly and forcefully challenging white privilege.

The letter yoyos from laudable to baffling statements. The bishops offer a beautiful reflection on the sin of racism and reiterate the calls for equality in housing and job opportunities expressed in the preceding pastoral. Yet in the bishops' discussion of European colonization, there is no mention of the Church's involvement and its need for repentance. The closest the pastoral comes to offering this is a generalized reflection on racism exhibited by Catholics:

> How great, therefore, is that sin of racism which weakens the Church's witness as the universal sign of unity among all peoples! How great the scandal given by racist Catholics who make the Body of Christ, the Church, a sign of racial oppression! Yet all too often the Church in our country has been for many a "white Church," a racist institution.

However, there are no action items aimed at reforming this racist institution.

The latter portion of the letter has quotes from the Scriptures, Church documents, and statements from Pope John Paul II, and while these beautiful words support the Church's stance against racism, they seem merely theoretical when juxtaposed with the bishops' gaping omissions in this document. That being said, the bishops offer a statement from *Gaudium et spes* that should be reflected on by every sitting bishop: "The Church... recognizes that worthy elements are found in today's social movements, especially an evolution toward unity, a process of wholesome socialization and of association in civic and economic realms" (40).

The letter calls for conversion from racism both as a personal sin (as in racial stereotypes, slurs, and jokes) and structural sin that deters "the economic, educational, and social advancement of the poor." Additionally, the bishops call on Catholics "at all levels" to examine their consciences "regarding attitudes and behavior toward blacks, Hispanics, Native Americans, and Asians." This is an important call but useless if not put into action. The U.S. bishops "urge consideration of the evil of racism as it exists in the local Church and reflection upon the means of combating it." However, minimal means are provided in or following the letter.

The bishops also "urge scrupulous attention at every level to ensure that minority representation goes beyond mere tokenism and involves authentic sharing in responsibility and decision making." This is another important call, and the bishops follow it by calling for the fostering of more vocations among nonwhite Catholics and greater diversity in the U.S. Church's hierarchy. However, since 88 percent of U.S. bishops are white, tokenism continues to be an issue.

The letter concludes urging that there "must be no turning back along the road of justice, no sighing for bygone times of privilege, no nostalgia for simple solutions from another age." Yet the reaction of white Catholics to the "browning" of the Church, the tendency to placate white Catholics rather than challenge them to confront their privilege and biases, and the persisting white hierarchy indicate that the U.S. Church is hanging onto the bygone times of colonization and white supremacy, the nostalgia of a Catholicism that pictures Jesus as a fair-skinned man with blue eyes and blonde hair, and the alignment of some white Catholics with alt-right politics suggest that the opposite is true. Thus, the U.S. Church is seeking to preserve and protect its whiteness. One only has to revisit

Empty Words and Empty Promises

Dolan's statement on Confederate statues to be convinced that the Church is attached to a heritage of white supremacy.

In my review, each of these three pastoral letters, while having nice words, great quotes, and lofty ideals, fail miserably in moving the Church "at all levels" against racism. Nearly forty years pass between *Brothers and Sisters to Us* and the next pastoral on racism. The U.S. Church devolved in its focus and attention on the sin of racism, treating it as a solved problem in a post-racial society. This is evident since ahead of the 2008 U.S. presidential election, when the USCCB was updating its official voting guide, one bishop proposed removing language that named racism as an intrinsic evil, citing the "progress" that has been made in society regarding racism.[11]

In its official document on voting, "Forming Consciences for Faithful Citizenship," the USCCB defined an intrinsically evil action as one that is deeply flawed and always opposed to the authentic good of persons since it is always incompatible with the love of God and neighbor (22). The document named abortion and euthanasia as examples of intrinsic evils. The nature of an intrinsic evil does not change if a society commits it less. The evil remains an evil.

However, this unnamed bishop clearly errs in his assessment that racism is no longer a major problem. Racism is an intrinsic evil since, like abortion and euthanasia, it is a sin predicated on an action that is deeply flawed, always opposed to the authentic good of persons, and always incompatible with the love of God and neighbor. One cannot love one's neighbor while thinking that the other's race is inferior. One cannot believe that God is Love (1 John 4:16), the God who made all persons in God's image and likeness, while professing that God created some people as less deserving of dignity and therefore less loveable.

Therefore, as an intrinsic evil racism cannot be considered as any less of an evil even if a society decreases in committing that evil, *whether the decrease is perceived or actual.* Many white Americans believe that racism is no longer a problem. The fact that a bishop said this and that as a result the USCCB agreed to remove racism as a named intrinsic evil reveals that there are many in the U.S. Catholic hierarchy who are blinded by their white privilege and ineffective as ministers of the gospel because of it.

The inability to forcefully name and denounce racism, especially its manifestations as white nationalism, white supremacy, and white privilege, continually recurs the Church's treatment of this disease. The U.S. bishops' cluelessness, blindness, and tone-deafness are inexcusable; their complicity with these named areas of racism appears to be a ticket to being a bishop in the U.S. Catholic Church, thereby promoting a barrier for the flourishing of nonwhite Catholics in the U.S. Church.

The presidency of Donald Trump revealed the prevalence of racism today. Amid the backdrop of the heightened racist rhetoric in both the society and in the Church and erupting with the Charlottesville Unite the Right rally in August of 2017 and the violent car attack there, warranted a long overdue response from the U.S. bishops. Alas, their inability to forcefully confront the problematic elements of Trump's election platform and his administration resulted in an unobstructed path for an emboldened and violent racism.

Open Wide Our Hearts (2018)

The pastoral *Open Wide Our Hearts* is longer than the USCCB's prior letters on racism. The first page begins with a definition of *racism* as both conscious and unconscious, but it ignores the fundamental truth of the *Imago Dei*. The bishops name examples of deliberate, sinful acts of racism to include racial profiling, "discrimination in hiring, housing, educational opportunities, and incarceration," Islamophobia, and the reappearance of symbols of hatred such as nooses and swastikas (4).

This last point requires a pause to discuss a significant backstory regarding the mention of "nooses and swastikas" in this pastoral. In a revelatory article in *Sojourners*, Dr. Eric Martin exposed that when the U.S. bishops met to draft this pastoral, Bishop Anthony Taylor of the Diocese of Little Rock, Arkansas, proposed an amendment to *condemn* swastikas, Confederate flags, and nooses.[12] While this amendment ought to have been unanimously and overwhelmingly accepted, the bishops rejected it, saying that swastikas and nooses were already "widely recognized signs of hatred," and decided to omit any mention of Confederate flags on the basis of this being a "sign of heritage," echoing Dolan's statement against taking down Confederate monuments and statues.

The failure to condemn all three of these racist images, especially the Confederate flag—the symbol of slavery, white supremacy, and the brutality and rape of Black bodies—is a failure of the USCCB in its witness to the gospel of Jesus Christ and its call to shepherd all people, not just whites. The bishops' refusal to condemn the Confederate flag furthers the U.S. Church's guilt in its cooperation with slavery and white supremacy. Rather than being a *mea culpa*, *Open Wide Our Hearts* reveals from the start that the U.S. bishops have hardened and empty hearts regarding the problem of racism and the oppression of the racially marginalized.

But the drama does not end there. After pressure from the USCCB and Catholic Charities USA, *Sojourners* retracted Martin's article.[13] *Sojourners*' founder and editor-in-chief Jim Wallis disclosed that the USCCB and Catholic Charities USA, among other organizations, had expressed "outrage"[14] over the publication of the article, with the implicit threat to pull funding for joint antipoverty initiatives. Rather than risk losing support for these initiatives, Wallis revealed his quandary as he made the "agonizing" decision to rescind the article.

By pressuring *Sojourners* to remove Martin's article, both the USCCB and Catholic Charities USA revealed their complicity in racism, along with their reaction of white fragility when called out on it. Both organizations negated the word *Catholic* in their names. Rather than witness to the universal dignity of *all* persons, the USCCB and Catholic Charities USA defended white nationalism and white supremacy.

The withdrawal of Martin's article was particularly troubling. The message conveyed by episcopal censorship is despotism toward the laity—do not criticize us or we will silence you—like the Church's historical message to victims of pedophilia and sexual abuse, and those protesting the death of unarmed Black man Eric Garner, whose last words were "I can't breathe," also uttered more than twenty times by the murdered George Floyd.

The surprising element in the removal of Martin's article was the involvement of Catholic Charities USA, which has historically advocated for justice for the poor and oppressed and offers a variety of gospel-oriented ministries, including but not limited to affordable housing, immigration and relief services, advocacy and social policy initiatives, and disaster services. Given Catholic Charities USA's mission and ministries, it appears antithetical for it to side with the USCCB's outrage over Miller's article.

However, the missing link in Catholic Charities USA's betrayal of its mission stems from the USCCB's lobbying efforts[15] to secure a path for Catholic parishes and organizations to be eligible for Payment Protection Program (PPP), which the U.S. Congress passed into law to provide immediate financing for businesses to pay their employees and fund overhead costs amid shutdowns and the decline in activity due to the coronavirus pandemic.

Empty Words and Empty Promises

Religious organizations would normally not be entitled to such government assistance given their tax-exempt status and religious purpose. However, lobbying by the USCCB provided Catholic organizations with unprecedented access to this government funding. Organizations within Catholic Charities USA were among the recipients of PPP loans, receiving as much as $220 million.[16] Therefore, Catholic Charities USA might have had a financial interest aligning itself with the USCCB in the outcry over Eric Martin's *Sojourners* article.

Wallis's decision had a strong impact on *Sojourners*. Two of its editors resigned: Daniel José Camacho and Dhanya Addanki, both individuals of color. In her resignation announcement on Twitter, Dhanya Addanki described herself as a "Dalit woman."[17] Dalits have been historically marginalized by India's caste system. Daniel José Camacho wrote, "It's become clear that I cannot stay here [at *Sojourners*] without compromising my own values and commitments to social justice, journalistic integrity, and honoring diverse and marginalized voices."[18]

This shakeup led to Wallis leaving his editorial role at *Sojourners* and the appointment of Sandi Villareal as its new editor-in-chief,[19] along with a commitment to editorial independence, which includes but is not limited to retaining any article that had been previously approved by *Sojourners*' editorial board. When Martin's article was returned to *Sojourners*' digital platform, there were numerous editorial notes on the article's removal, reinstatement, and further apologies. It was an embarrassing moment in journalism.

Following the removal of his article, Martin released a response: "The removal of my article from *Sojourners*' website underlines the profound need for Catholics to address overt and covert white supremacist cultures within our Church."[20] Martin's article and response represents the prophetic call, rooted in Baptism, to promote the *Imago Dei*, defend the racially marginalized, and unmask forces of oppression. Prophets are silenced, but God is with them and prevails in the end.

After expanding on this fault in *Open Wide Our Hearts*, it might be reasonable to discard the entire pastoral. In fact, Fr. Dan Horan described it as a "worthless statement."[21] However, for the sake of offering a comprehensive and prophetic response to the letter, let us continue our critical review of the document.

The letter identifies the presence of both conscious and unconscious racism, the latter "placed there unwillingly or unknowingly by our upbringing and culture. As such, it can lead to thoughts and actions that we do not even see as racist, but nonetheless flow from the same prejudicial root" (5). The bishops acknowledge that racism causes objective harm even if subjectively an individual does not intend on such harm. The beliefs themselves are harmful and can result in the vilification of certain races and ethnicities, as Donald Trump did Mexicans. The bishops note that even unconscious beliefs can make one an accomplice to racism.

As a supplement to *Open Wide Our Hearts*, the USCCB's website provides a companion worksheet on unconscious bias.[22] While brief, this is a positive step to promote a means for the faithful to further examine themselves and discern how the sin of racism has been intertwined in their upbringing and formation, unbeknownst to them, and how they can discern and root out subtle thought patterns and habits that promote inequity.

On social media, a recently ordained priest challenged me on the validity of unconscious bias and cited a "scholarly" podcast interview with Coleman Hughes, a Black writer for multiple right-of-center publications. I pointed out to the priest the statement from *Open Wide Our Hearts* on subconscious bias, and that swiftly ended the exchange. It appears this priest had not read this pastoral letter and had not heard of it. This suggests a gap in seminary education, not only on racial ethics but on the USCCB's own documents.

The bishops admit that while society has made progress regarding racism, "racism still profoundly affects our culture, and it has no place in the Christian heart. This evil causes great harm to its victims, and it corrupts the souls of those who harbor racist or prejudicial thoughts. The persistence of the evil of racism is why we are writing this letter now. People are still being harmed, so action is still needed" (6–7).

To combat racism, the bishops state that every one of us is called to a genuine conversion of heart, with the aim that conversion be not only personal but institutional. They acknowledge the gap in catechesis, as too "many good and faithful Catholics remain unaware of the connection between institutional racism and the continued erosion of the sanctity of life" (10). Additionally, the bishops exhort that Christians are called to listen and know the stories of their brothers and sisters, and to allow our hearts to be moved with both compassion and the desire for justice.

The letter includes the historical oppression of Native Americans, Blacks, and Latin Americans. The bishops practically omit the Church's complicity in each group's respective experience, but they summarize the Church's cooperation in slavery (21), blocking of Indigenous clergy, and promotion of segregated parishes (22). They admit this sin and ask for forgiveness. The faithful too are called upon to examine their consciences.

The following, toward the end of the pastoral, could be one of its most enriching statements, touching on the one area into which present-day bishops are reluctant to enter:

> To work at ending racism, we need to engage the world and encounter others—to see, maybe for the first time, those who are on the peripheries of our own limited view. Knowing that the Lord has taken the divine initiative by loving us first, we can boldly

go forward, reaching out to others. We must invite into dialogue those we ordinarily would not seek out. We must work to form relationships with those we might regularly try to avoid. This demands that we go beyond ourselves, opening our minds and hearts to value and respect the experiences of those who have been harmed by the evil of racism. (23)

Sadly, the bishops do not seem willing to engage, for instance, the co-foundresses of the Black Lives Matter Global Network, but this is exactly what the pastoral is calling for—and the USCCB ostensibly pledges to do—to dialogue with those they ordinarily would not seek out. One of the BLM co-foundresses, Patrisse Cullors, lives in Los Angeles. Could Archbishop Gómez put the pastoral into practice and have a listening session with Ms. Cullors and her associates? Could Bishop Barron, formerly the auxiliary for the Santa Barbara region, join in rather than embracing right-wing ideologies and critiquing BLM from afar?

What comes across most emphatically in *Open Wide Our Hearts*, along with the previous pastorals, is the hypocrisy of the U.S. bishops, resulting in little progress in terms of racism and the U.S. Church. Until the bishops practice what they preach, boldly and directly call out white supremacy (and white supremacists), engage in real dialogue with marginalized communities and secular social justice movements, and reflect more diversity along with greater investment of resources in multicultural ministries, every pastoral letter on racism will be empty words and promises. The bishops fail as credible and prophetic witnesses to Christ's call to preach the gospel to all nations (see Matt 28:19) if they are unwilling to uphold, not just in theory but in practice, the dignity of all peoples.

Dan Horan sums up what is needed in a USCCB pastoral letter on racism:

Empty Words and Empty Promises

> The church in the US needs a document that does not spare the feelings or prioritize the comfort of white people like me. The reality of racism requires an honest acknowledgement of the basic truth that racism is a white problem and progress will only be made when church leaders accept and preach this fact.[23]

In other words, a pastoral on racism will be ineffective unless it is willing to make the 88 percent white bishops and the white members of the U.S. Church uncomfortable. This is the necessary path to conversion, particularly to surrender attachment to privilege—the antithesis to the cross of Christ. As Shane Claiborne famously stated, "God comforts the disturbed and disturbs the comfortable."[24]

Therefore, to witness to Christ and defend the racially marginalized, the bishops must call on white Catholics to deny themselves and their fragility and leave behind their comfort and privilege to work for justice for those who are truly and unjustly disturbed. Without this, the U.S. Church perpetuates the attack on the dignity of the racially oppressed. Rather than be united with the crucified Lord, a Church that wavers in its solidarity with those who are harmed due to their ethnicity leaves the Body of Christ scarred and abandoned.

6

RESTORING AND REBUILDING THE DIVIDED HOUSE

Unless the Lord build the house,
they labor in vain who build.

—Psalm 127:1

As if gazing on the aftermath of the destruction of a large building, we look upon the shambles of the divided U.S. Church with shock, horror, sadness, and anger. However, as they say in the Cursillo movement: *Who is the Church? We are the Church!* Most of the Body of Christ is made up of the laity. Yet power is concentrated in the hands of the ordained few.

Even so, God gives each of the baptized a prophetic call, and no ordained man has power that supersedes that of the Holy Trinity. Thus, we the laity call upon the U.S. hierarchy to be still and surrender to the voice of God. There is no moving forward without listening to the Spirit, often manifest in the lowly. What must the bishops do to move forward with God? Here are eight recommendations that can lead to reconciliation, healing, and wholeness in the U.S. Catholic Church.

1. Actions Speak Louder than Words

The four pastoral letters from the U.S. bishops on racism contain many nice, encouraging, and at times exhortative words. However, on many occasions the bishops' actions contradicted their words. Talk is cheap. Actions speak louder than words. As St. Ignatius of Loyola says in his Spiritual Exercises, "Love ought to manifest itself in deeds rather than in words" (230). What deeds ought the U.S. Catholic bishops manifest?

First of all, they must be credible witnesses and practice what they preach. *Gaudium et spes* and *The National Race Crisis* call for the Church to cooperate with social movements and civic groups. It's time for the bishops to put this in practice rather than vilifying organizations such as BLM. They should learn more about the BLM movement, particularly from its leaders, and find areas for collaboration in the common mission of promoting the dignity of Black lives. They ought to put aside their biases and put into practice the invocation in *Open Wide Our Hearts* to "invite into dialogue those we ordinarily would not seek out" and "work to form relationships with those we might regularly try to avoid."

The U.S. bishops need not look far to learn how to practice what they preach. Following the killing of George Floyd, Bishop Mark Seitz of El Paso, Texas, and twelve priests from the diocese knelt together at El Paso's Memorial Park in solidarity in response to this tragic event.[1] They also held signs stating "BLM" and "Black Lives Matter." Seitz and his priests chose this location since the day before, protestors and police clashed at that site.[2] The El Paso clergy present prayed for eight minutes, the length of time Officer Derek Chauvin had his knee on George Floyd's neck.

This gesture spoke volumes to both Catholics and non-Catholics, but especially to Pope Francis. After Bishop Seitz's witness, the pope called him to acknowledge his efforts toward solidarity and racial justice. Seitz commented, "I expressed to the Holy Father that I felt it was imperative to show our solidarity to those who are suffering."[3] By this act, Pope Francis is signaling the U.S. bishops that Bishop Seitz's demonstration is the type of witness and action he would like to see from the rest of them.

The U.S. bishops should act in ways that are consistent with the Holy Father's message regarding George Floyd and the racial justice protests. During a general audience, Pope Francis prayed "for the repose of the soul of George Floyd and of all those others who have lost their lives as a result of the sin of racism." The pope called on Catholics not to "tolerate or turn a blind eye to racism and exclusion in any form."[4] Additionally, Pope Francis mentioned George Floyd by name twice in *Let Us Dream*, supporting the racial justice protests following his death:

> There is another abuse of power which we saw in the horrendous police killing of George Floyd that triggered protests around the world against racial injustice. It is right that people reclaim the dignity of every human being from abuse in all of its forms. Abuse is a gross violation of human dignity that we cannot allow and which we must continue to struggle against.
>
> To know ourselves as a people is to be aware of something greater that unites us, something that cannot be reduced to a shared legal or physical identity. We saw this in the protests in reaction to the killing of George Floyd, when many people who otherwise did not know each other took to the streets to protest, united by a healthy indignation. Such movements reveal not just popular feeling but the feeling of a people, its "soul."[5]

Pope Francis supports racial justice protests and solidarity movements that call for an end of racially motivated violence. How difficult would it be for the U.S. bishops to do the same? Francis makes an even bolder declaration by connecting the protests against George Floyd's death with the Good Samaritan.[6] If Pope Francis names the protestors "collective Samaritans,"[7] then who are the bishops imitating when they do not act, look the other way, and attack social justice movements?

Thus, the U.S. bishops cannot remain bystanders amid the persistence of racial oppression. Rather, they ought to learn from the protestors and participate in the call to be collective Samaritans by collaborating with social movements—practicing what was preached in the Church documents. Credibility is certainly an issue for the U.S. bishops. To rebuild their divided and wrecked house, they must show love in deeds more than words.

2. Listen to Black Catholics Voices, Particularly Black Theologians, Writers, and Activists

If the U.S. bishops truly do not want to disenfranchise Black Catholics, they ought to take the time to engage with them rather than give speeches attacking movements that defend their rights, while simultaneously doing little to promote and protect Black lives. There are many Black Catholics the bishops could dialogue with. Bryan Massingale's *Racial Justice and the Catholic Church* ought to be required reading for every member of the clergy. The laity too can benefit from it. Should the bishops wish to seriously address racism, they need to include Massingale in this process. The USCCB Ad Hoc Committee on Racism must be in dialogue with him.

THE CATHOLIC CHURCH AND THE STRUGGLE FOR RACIAL JUSTICE

Perhaps the U.S. bishops are not open to Massingale because he challenged them to confront their own privilege.[8] Massingale calls for a radical response from the bishops to eradicate the evil of racism, and for Catholic catechesis and formation (especially priestly formation) to incorporate a theology and praxis to counter persistent racial oppression both inside and outside the Church. Some Catholics push back against Massingale partly because he publicly identifies as a member of the LGBTQ community.[9] But as *Open Wide Our Hearts* challenged, the U.S. Church must be willing to dialogue with people they would normally exclude from the conversation.

In addition, the bishops ought to dialogue with Olga Segura, an Afro-Latinx woman who has written for and edited multiple Catholic publications. In 2021, Ms. Segura published *Birth of a Movement: Black Lives Matter and the Catholic Church*. Along with Massingale's, Segura's book ought to be required reading for Catholics, especially members of the clergy, especially since many of the ordained hold an antagonistic view of the BLM movement, whether they express it publicly or privately.

Segura challenges the bishops to do the following:

1. Issue a formal pastoral letter addressing the harm done to Black people by the Church, from slavery to inconsistent and tone-deaf responses to police brutality, and apologize for the Church's complicity in white supremacy and failure to publicly minister to Black people.
2. Acknowledge that Church leaders, who are mostly white men, benefit from privileges not afforded to Blacks and other people of color.
3. Reflect on how this privilege prevents Church leaders from seeing brutality and the oppression of Black people, and call on white priests and donors to also engage in this exercise.

4. Work to keep Black members in the Church, by listening to their cries and declaring that the Church is committed to Black liberation by supporting BLM.
5. Build a safe place for Black people in the Church by condemning all racial harm, from belittlement to police brutality.[10]

Like Massingale, Segura calls on the bishops to acknowledge their own complicity and to challenge white Catholics rather than continue to appease and protect them from recognizing their privilege and their need to actively combat racism.

The U.S. bishops can no longer ignore the three million Black Catholics living in the United States.[11] While this might not be the strongest donor base, the assets of the Church are in its people—not in bank accounts. As long as the U.S. Church continues to turn away from Black Catholics, it will promote injustice toward them.

The Church's injustice to Black Catholics is exemplified by the lack of fully canonized Black Catholic saints. Alejandra Molina observes, "Out of the more than 10,000 men and women recognized as saints, which includes 11 Americans and a total of 899 that have been canonized by Francis, none are African Americans." This implies, if unintentionally, that there are no Black Catholic holy men and women worthy of mention, and that saintliness is not a characteristic of the Black community. If anything, the reverse is true. Those who experience oppression and injustice bear within them deep and real holiness. Real saints do not have halos, they have scars. True saints are those who were without honor while alive.

As Black Catholic activist and East Baltimore resident Ralph Moore comments, the Church ought to "recognize the hardships African American Catholics have endured over the years— being expected to sit in the back of the church or receiving

THE CATHOLIC CHURCH AND THE STRUGGLE FOR RACIAL JUSTICE

Communion only after white Catholics had done so." Moore also notes how tone-deaf and embarrassing the Church appears for not elevating Black Catholics to sainthood thus far: "They don't see us. We're like hidden members and they need to learn how to see us."

The U.S. and global Church must begin to see Black Catholics and the Black community. For far too long, the Church has averted its eyes, treating with disdain a group that truly and fully bears the *Imago Dei*. By doing this, the Church sides with the oppressors and persecutors, not with the oppressed and persecuted, and so it does not stand with Christ.

Black Catholic parishes are often more welcoming than any other Roman Catholic parishes. They treat newcomers, even Catholics who are not Black, like one of their own. Black Catholics have a history of generational stories that cannot go unheard. Rather than deem them as unworthy of holiness, Black Catholics are icons of the suffering, rejected, spat upon, and persecuted Christ. It is time for the Church to give its Black members their due.

Finally, the U.S. bishops need to pay heed to the National Black Catholic Clergy Caucus (NBCCC) and the National Black Sisters' Conference (NBSC). The NBCCC's inaugural meeting in 1968 challenged the U.S. bishops, leading them to pen *The National Race Crisis*. In particular, the NBCCC famously classified the U.S. Church as a "white racist institution"[12] and a home for their oppressors who in turn treat Black Catholics as "second rate."[13] Regrettably, this treatment by the U.S. Church continues.

I want to draw particular focus to the National Black Sisters' Conference. Black women were excluded from Catholic religious orders and were subject to the oppression of segregation.[14] Out of this painful history of inequity and injustice, the National Black Sisters' Conference wrote a response to Archbishop Gómez's November 4, 2021, address.

Restoring and Rebuilding the Divided House

The NBSC rightfully chastised Gómez and called him out for not acting "in solidarity with those who have suffered at the hands of white supremacy since first being kidnapped from their homeland and enslaved with the blessing of the Catholic Church....For the most part, you have remained mysteriously and regretfully silent; often failing to call out hate groups for their racist ideologies and violence."[15] The sisters called on Gómez to rethink his remarks, and invited him to meet with them and dialogue on race relations. Sadly, he did not respond to the NBSC's invitation. Such inaction by the president of the USCCB affirms the belief that Black Catholics are treated as second rate, and that the U.S. Church is a white racist institution.

3. Listen to and Become Informed by Experts in the Field of Racism

In the spirit of collaborating with civic organizations and dialoguing with those normally excluded from the conversation, the U.S. bishops ought to consult with and learn from experts on racism. Ibram X. Kendi's timely book *How to Be an Antiracist* would be an extremely helpful resource to inform the bishops about racial justice. Kendi's wisdom could aid the bishops to better discern their own biases and history of socialization in racism, as well as learn the importance of working to promote policies and practices that foster equity for the racially marginalized. Robin DiAngelo is another expert whose wisdom could benefit the bishops, particularly her work and research on *White Fragility: Why It's So Hard for White People to Talk about Racism*. The title says it all, especially since the U.S. Church has been reluctant in tackling racism head-on for fear of alienating its white members.

Some believe the Church ought to only consider religious texts for information on racism. Clearly the clergy sex abuse crisis made it clear that the Church needs to look beyond "religion" to understand and address its grave ills. It needs the grace of humility to admit that it has fallen short in combatting racism and accept assistance and guidance from experts. Without this humility, the U.S. Church will remain divided.

4. Listen to and Learn from the Laity

In addition to seeking the humility to accept direction from known experts on racism, the U.S. bishops need to listen to and learn from the laity who are effectively and diligently working for racial justice. The pedantic, condescending tone of Bishop Barron in his article "Why 'What Are the Bishops Doing about It' Is the Wrong Question" highlights how mistaken and unaware they are of how far they have strayed from aligning themselves with the racially marginalized by not collaborating with lay movements. The U.S. bishops ought to follow the example of the laity's activism in response to the injustices enacted on George Floyd, Breonna Taylor, and so many others.

The U.S. bishops should let lay activists teach them how to have hearts formed with love for the racially marginalized and with a passion to defend and support them. They shouldn't be afraid to get their black suits dirty and join the laity in taking a knee in solidarity with the slain George Floyd and all who fear a similar fate. Otherwise the bishops remain bystanders, walking past their neighbors beaten and lying in a ditch.

5. Cooperate with Local Movements

Bishops need to have their eyes and ears opened to how racial injustice is occurring in their respective dioceses, and act. When the bishops only address the people in the pews who pay

Restoring and Rebuilding the Divided House

their tithe, they neglect the rest of God's people. Christ called on his disciples to attend to the lost sheep outside the fold (see Matt 18:10–14). However, when it comes to racial injustice, more than one sheep is alienated and left unprotected.

In Los Angeles County, a Black family, the Bruces, owned beachfront land in picturesque Manhattan Beach. The family created a safe place for Black people to enjoy the beach, and attracted attacks from the Ku Klux Klan, which attempted to burn their property.[16] The city of Manhattan Beach wrongfully seized the Bruces' land by eminent domain in 1929.[17] Following the death of George Floyd, and upon learning of the injustice done to a Black family in her city, activist Kavon Ward and several others formed Justice for Bruce's Beach to call for the return of the unjustly seized land to the descendants of the Bruce family.[18]

Although Manhattan Beach resisted the efforts of Ms. Ward and her fellow activists, Justice for Bruce's Beach gained the attention of Los Angeles County Supervisor Janice Hahn, who highlighted the need for legislation to return the land to its rightful owners.[19] On September 30, 2021, California Governor Gavin Newsom signed Senate Bill 796 into law, authorizing the return of the Bruces' land to the descendants.[20]

When the activism for the Bruce family was heating up, I asked Ms. Ward if the Manhattan Beach Catholic parish expressed solidarity with the call for justice for the Bruces. No. Nor did the Archdiocese of Los Angeles show any support. When someone who is not Catholic observes the lack of response from the Church on a matter that affects the validity of equal rights predicated on intrinsic human dignity, the Church communicates that it does not defend the racially marginalized and is indifferent to their suffering.

The Church cannot and must not remain a bystander. Rather, it must join the "collective Samaritans" in courageously, compassionately, and unabashedly siding with the racially marginalized, the ones beaten and left on the side of the road. If the U.S. Church wishes to become a credible witness, it must exhibit a generosity of heart that will go forth and be with the racially oppressed.

6. Address Catholics Who Benefit from White Assimilation and White Privilege

In the first half of the twentieth century and before, European immigrants ranging from Irish, Italian, Polish, and Eastern European were the victims of ethnic prejudice.[21] Compounding this, European *Catholic* immigrants were targeted by Protestant nativists. The Ku Klux Klan hated Catholic immigrants, and as a result Catholic parishes and other institutions such as convents were vandalized.[22] Nativists portrayed Italian immigrants as inferior to those of Northern European heritage and caricatured them as criminals.[23]

Like the slur wielded against BLM activists and social justice proponents, Nativists claimed Italian and Eastern European immigrants were socialists.[24] These immigrants became scapegoats, and like Black Americans, subject to lynching.[25] Nativists stereotyped Irish immigrants as drunkards, lazy, violent, and subhuman.[26] Irish immigrants were often relegated to dangerous, menial, and low-paying jobs. Businesses posted signs stating, "No Irish Need Apply,"[27] and they took these jobs because they had no other choice. With rhetoric resembling President Trump's dismissal of Mexicans, James Silk Buckingham described Irish immigrants as "drunken, dirty, indolent and riotous, so as to be objects of fear and dislike to all."[28]

In the eighteenth century, French colonists living in Nova Scotia who refused to take an oath of allegiance to Great Britain were expelled from Canada, and many of them sent to America.[29] The deported, known as Acadians or "Cajuns," became indentured servants and beggars in the United States, many eventually settling in the swamplands of Louisiana.[30] Cajuns were ridiculed and discriminated against for speaking French, for their accent and cuisine, and jokes ridiculing them were common.[31]

European immigrants before and into the twentieth century stood at the crossroads: choose between assimilation with the predominant white culture or maintain their ethnic identity, potentially aligning themselves with Persons of Color. They and their descendants "chose whiteness and sought to demonstrate their cultural and biological fitness."[32] Marco Tabellini and Vicky Fouka demonstrated that immigrants whose culture and physical appearance were closer to Nativists (and who were willing to adapt and become like the Nativists) were more successful at assimilation.[33] Thus, descendants of European immigrants, a category of people who were once hated by "native" Americans, cooperated with the social schema to be accepted into the "white race," benefiting over time from the privileges of being white.

Reviewing the history of ridicule and discrimination against European immigrants should remind us of the attacks on the dignity of today's immigrants. The U.S. Church has an opportunity here. Catholics of Italian, Irish, Portuguese, and Eastern European descent need to reflect on their history in the United States. Recalling how their predecessors were persecuted could lead them to understand the need to express care for and solidarity with the racially marginalized.

The U.S. bishops need to call white Catholics away from the comfort and privilege of assimilation and into the margins with the oppressed. They need to recognize that while Nativists harmed their European predecessors, and that they as Catholics cannot stand by while their Black, Brown, and Asian/Pacific

Islander brothers and sisters are attacked. Moreover, the U.S. bishops need to address the white privilege of all white Catholics, whether or not they are descendants of formerly persecuted European ethnic groups.

7. Desist from Protecting and Harboring Racists

The U.S. bishops cannot credibly promote racial justice if they remain silent when faced with racism, particularly among Catholics (especially prominent ones). Then-Archbishop Wilton Gregory was the only bishop who called out Trump[34] for his bogus photo op that resulted in tear gas lobbed at protestors.[35] Most of his brother bishops remained silent while Trump used racial epithets against Mexicans, Native Americans,[36] Asians,[37] Muslims,[38] Blacks,[39] East Indians,[40] and others. Trump described Haiti and African countries using coarse, derogatory language,[41] and antagonized Black and Brown female members of Congress.[42] In addition, Trump's allies include white supremacists, including Richard Spencer[43] and the Proud Boys.[44]

When the bishops are bystanders while a sitting president spouts racial hatred, they signal that BIPOC Catholics do not matter. The bishops remain silent as prominent Catholics espouse racism. Representative Steve King reportedly displayed a Confederate flag on his congressional desk[45] and has promoted white supremacist rhetoric.[46] Former Attorney General Bill Barr, a Catholic who was honored at the National Catholic Prayer Breakfast in 2020 with the Christifideles Laici Award (with Bishop Barron delivering the keynote address),[47] denies the existence of systemic racism in the justice system.[48] The bishops rebuked neither of them. James Altman, a controversial priest whose bishop removed him from his parish, banned him from preaching, and restricted him to only celebrating private Masses,[49] questioned the reality of the lynching of Black persons.[50] Yet Altman carries on freely, spouting his hatred.[51] The Church can no longer harbor racists. Racism by Catholics continues because it goes unchecked by priests and bishops.

A cursory review of social media reveals how prevalent racism is among self-described Catholics, particularly anonymous accounts that often sport profile pictures of a holy image or saint. Whenever I have challenged racism online, including calling Catholics to give up racism for Lent in 2020,[52] I received an onslaught of attacks. The same happened when I questioned if Our Lady of Guadalupe would be received if she appeared to members of the U.S. Church today.[53] Until the bishops condemn racism as consistently as they do abortion, the U.S. Church will continue to be a home for racists.

8. Reaffirm that Racism Is an *Intrinsic Evil*

Following the bishops' 2008 statement, incidents in U.S. society continued to prove that racism is a pressing problem. As we saw in part 1, however, racism is a sin and a heresy that denies the intrinsic dignity of the human person formed in the *Imago Dei*. The USCCB must name racism as an intrinsic evil. To do otherwise perpetuates it.

As demonstrated by the murders of George Floyd, Breonna Taylor, and so many others, racism does not only diminish one's inherent dignity to the point of death, but it also renders such a death as inconsequential.

Conclusion

The prophetic call to demand accountability from the U.S. bishops for racism is reminiscent of the dialogue between the prophet Nathan and King David (see Sam 12:1–12). Nathan told David about a rich man who took a poor man's only ewe and fed it to a traveler. Hearing this angered David, but he soon learned that he had done the same when he robbed Uriah of his wife Bathsheba to satisfy his own lust.

Like Nathan, inspired by the prophetic gift from God, we call on the bishops to respond like David when confronted with this truth from Nathan: "I have sinned against the Lord" (2 Sam 12:13). The U.S. bishops need to beg God for forgiveness and confess to the people of God that they have failed in defending the *Imago Dei* in the racially marginalized. They cannot point to their pastoral letters—empty words with empty promises, followed by inaction. Every bishop needs to respond to racism physically and spiritually like Bishop Mark Seitz did—unapologetically, unambiguously, and unabashedly. They must reverence God by respecting the *Imago Dei* in every person, and defending it when it is denied in a person or group of people.

It is time for the U.S. bishops to repent and take this opportunity to learn about racism from those who experience it. The white 88 percent of the U.S. bishops can educate themselves on white privilege and take accountability for the injustices borne by those without this privilege. Finally, the bishops must dialogue with theologians and activists, both in and outside the Church, and collaborate on the shared goal of protecting and defending the dignity of all people. We don't need more pastoral letters. We need pastoral activity.

In the next chapter, we will discuss the growing conservative trend in the U.S. Catholic Church, beginning during John Paul II's pontificate and gaining momentum under Benedict

XVI. This movement fostered the Culture Wars, narrowing the faith into a single issue while evading the Church's responsibility in other critical areas. Just as racism causes a division in the Body of Christ, the Culture Wars promote division in the American Church.

7
THE U.S. CHURCH IN THE THIRD MILLENNIUM

Beginning with John Paul II's pontificate, more conservative-leaning Catholics arose, particularly among Generation X and older millennials. The first World Youth Day held in North America and in an English-speaking nation took place in Denver, Colorado, in 1993. The visit from John Paul II had a profound effect on U.S. Catholics and one can trace the shift in ideology within this group and region to this.

This shift is not necessarily bad in itself. The uniqueness of regional Catholics should be appreciated as long as it is not detrimental to their union with the broader Church. American Catholics have a particular experience of the faith, given our unique societal dynamics and demographics, coupled with the added dimension of a growing Catholic population with roots in Mexico, Central and South America, the Caribbean, Vietnam, the Philippines, India, and Sri Lanka.

The trend of U.S. Catholics toward both appreciating their unique identity and growing in their love for the pope and Rome was welcome. As Aristotle says, however, moral virtue is the mean between two extremes.[1] During the pontificates of John Paul II and Benedict XVI, American Catholicism witnessed a rise in right-leaning ideology. There was a shift away from guitar liturgies to formal choirs, the emphasis on devotional practices outside of Mass, including but not limited to eucharistic adoration and public recitation of the Rosary, preaching that promoted Catholic orthodoxy and conservative values, and longer lines for the confessional. While there were certainly parishes that kept contemporary music along with "feel-good" preaching, there appeared to be a steady rise in parish piety.

Once again, this is not bad in itself. If anything, the universality of the Church ought to foster various forms of practice. Some young Catholics benefit by attending daily Mass, participating in eucharistic adoration and recitation of the Rosary, and frequent trips to the confessional, but such a narrow focus can lead to disengagement from others. Prayer and piety must follow the flow of the Trinity. God does not remain in an internal communion. As Karl Rahner said, "The economic Trinity *is* the immanent Trinity and vice versa."[2] God's love goes forth to humanity, as perfectly emulated in the incarnation. Our prayer is not for the purpose of navel-gazing but to call us out of ourselves to those in need.

The division fomented among some Catholics is often referred to as the "culture wars." I believe language from John Paul II's *Evangelium Vitae* inadvertently contributed to this when he spoke of a dichotomy between the "culture of death" (12) and the "culture of life" (50).

The culture of death is truly ignoble. This is "fostered by powerful cultural, economic and political currents which encourage an idea of society excessively concerned with efficiency" that disregards those labeled in society as the disabled, the ill and elderly, and those considered weak (12). This is identical to Pope Francis's exhortation against "throw away" culture (*EG* 53).

THE CATHOLIC CHURCH AND THE STRUGGLE FOR RACIAL JUSTICE

The culture of life is, simply put, the proclamation of the gospel of Jesus Christ with our words and our lives. Amid the prevailing societal norm to disregard the weak, John Paul II calls on Catholics to counteract such a trend and in the name of Jesus take a stand against this harmful tendency.

Twenty-six years later, the pope's message is still relevant. The deaths of Ahmaud Arbery, Breonna Taylor, and George Floyd are the result of the culture of death, which promotes the idea that the lives of certain people do not matter. Structural inequity that especially harms Black and Brown people is also symptomatic of the culture of death.

Unfortunately, the culture wars do not support movements that promote the dignity of Black lives or promote the comprehensive position on the weak and vulnerable that both John Paul II and Francis uphold. Rather, the "culture of life," at least in the American Church, boiled down to merely a *war on abortion*. The abortion discourse overtook and dominated American Catholicism, much more than Rome ever intended.

The 1974 Declaration on Procured Abortion called on Catholics to oppose not just the practice of abortion but the conditions that make abortion an attractive option. Inherent in the document is a moral imperative to give children every opportunity to be welcome. The Church therefore has expressed concern for the child after birth as well as before birth (23). This echoes what Archbishop Christophe Pierre, apostolic nuncio to the United States, declared to the U.S. bishops in November 2021:

> The Church must be unapologetically pro-life. We cannot abandon our defense of innocent human life or the vulnerable person. Yet, a synodal approach to the question would be to understand better why people seek to end pregnancies; what are the root causes of choices against life and what are the factors that make those choices so complicated for some; and, to

begin to form a consensus with concrete strategies to build the culture of life and the civilization of love.[3]

Consistent with John Paul II's comprehensive view of the weak and vulnerable, the document offers the following:

> Any discrimination based on the various stages of life is no more justified than any other discrimination. The right to life remains complete in an old person, even one greatly weakened; it is not lost by one who is incurably sick. The right to life is no less to be respected in the small infant just born than in the mature person. In reality, respect for human life is called for from the time that the process of generation begins. (12)

During a homily on January 27, 1999, in St. Louis, Missouri, Pope John Paul II unconditionally defined being pro-life as standing against euthanasia, the death penalty, and racism, working to eradicate "every form of racism, a plague which…[is] of the most persistent and destructive evils of the nation" (5).

In the 2018 apostolic exhortation *Gaudete et exsultate*, Pope Francis proclaimed that the unborn and the already born are equally sacred (101). Additionally, Pope Francis, responding to the death of George Floyd, stated "we cannot tolerate or turn a blind eye to racism and exclusion in any form and yet claim to defend the sacredness of every human life."[4] Thus, every human life, unborn and born, is sacred. This is an absolute, stemming from the *Imago Dei* being in all persons.

Bryan Massingale describes this single-issue focus as an "American aberration" that is "a cover for anti-Blackness and racism."[5] He continues that the Church in the United States, as a corporate body, "hides behind the rhetoric of being pro-life and using that language to mute concern over white nationalism."[6]

THE CATHOLIC CHURCH AND THE STRUGGLE FOR RACIAL JUSTICE

Massingale highlights the narrow interpretation of "pro-life" espoused by conservative U.S. Catholic leaders, who promote the defense of the unborn but remain silent on the value of Black and Brown lives, or even attack the idea as divisive.

Single-issue Catholicism is a severe problem in the U.S. Church and a deviation from *Evangelium Vitae*, but we cannot let Pope John Paul II off the hook too easily when he promotes a Manichean dualism with his imagery of culture war:

> This situation, with its lights and shadows, ought to make us all fully aware that we are facing an enormous and dramatic clash between good and evil, death and life, the "culture of death" and the "culture of life." We find ourselves not only "faced with" but necessarily "in the midst of" this conflict: we are all involved and we all share in it, with the inescapable responsibility of choosing to be unconditionally pro-life. (28)

Additionally, the pope uses the image of "a war of the powerful against the weak" (12), furthering the image of conflict in the previous quote. Whether he intended to or not, Pope John Paul II set up the culture wars, and the American Church not only ran with it, but focused itself on a single, antiabortion aim.

As we will see in the next chapter, a coalition of clergy, wealthy donors, and a burgeoning Catholic media empire not only fomented the culture wars but continues to promote an environment hostile to racial justice, and thereby permitting and propagating racism. This coalition fosters an idolatry of an American Catholic Church that truly and solely reflects a white Catholic Church, but there is only one Catholic Church, one that is truly universal—honoring and encouraging the diversity of the global, multicultural Body of Christ. All other so-called iterations of the Church are mere counterfeits.

8

A COALITION OF CLERGY AND LAITY AGAINST SOCIAL JUSTICE

> No one can serve two masters. He will either hate one and love the other, or be devoted to one and despise the other. You cannot serve God and mammon.
>
> —Matthew 6:24

Let us revisit Aidan McAleenan's statement: "I think it's about this, if you're going to be really honest about it, money, at the end of the day."[1] Wars are funded; culture wars are no different. Funding is a prerequisite to ensure the intended outcome. As Tom Roberts has noted,

> Paralleling the ascendancy of the Religious Right out of 1980s evangelicalism, today's Catholic Right is rising and well-financed. While pendulum swings are common between conservative and progressive tendencies in Catholicism, the 35-year traditionalist

reign of popes John Paul II and Benedict XVI allowed the Far Right to flourish.[2]

The "Far Right" is comprised of American bishops, priests, wealthy laypeople, and entities under their control. They are collectively aligned in their conservative positions and wish to inject them into the American Catholic Church, with reverberations in the global Church. This coalition can be linked to a parallel church or a "new US magisterium."[3] As stated earlier, when money talks, the bishops listen.

Roberts even notes that the Catholic Right has such staunch support from like-minded prelates that their coalition is "an alternative to the U.S. bishops' conference."[4] As Christ teaches us in the Scripture passage at the beginning of this chapter, however, our allegiance to God can be thwarted by a competing idol: money. The ecumenical movement of conservative Americans promotes a theology that evades and ignores the warnings to the rich and the exhortation to love and attend to the poor. Inclusive of this, while the Catholic Right might not call themselves believers in the Prosperity Gospel, the trajectory of their belief system says otherwise.

How does prioritizing certain ideologies over the gospel become so fluidly espoused by Catholic clergy and laity who, on the surface, are faithful to the Church? Who is Jesus to them when they omit his Beatitude "Blessed are you who are poor" (Luke 6:20) and "Amen, I say to you, it will be hard for one who is rich to enter the kingdom of heaven" (Matt 19:23)?

As I mentioned in the previous chapter, St. Ignatius of Loyola teaches us that the evil spirit disguises itself as an Angel of Light (Spiritual Exercises, 332) who offers "holy and pious thoughts that are wholly in conformity with the sanctity of the soul" until this Angel of Light endeavors "little by little to end by drawing the soul into his hidden snares and designs."

A Coalition of Clergy and Laity against Social Justice

A coalition of clergy and wealthy donors, under the guise of promoting Christian principles such as respect for marriage and family, along with the right to life for the unborn, have prioritized *their* magisterium and *their* agenda over that of Jesus Christ and his *Catholic* Church. By siding with the rich, this coalition loses touch with the poor who are so close to Christ. It is no wonder then that any movement that supports the marginalized, many of whom are nonwhite, does not coalesce with the Catholic Right. In fact, social justice movements and attention toward the poor threatens their paper-thin, dollar-funded magisterium. Who are the members of this coalition?

Eternal Word Television Network (EWTN)

Let us begin with an apostolate that began with God's grace building on the enterprising nature from an unlikely agent: a cloistered, Poor Clare nun. In the twentieth century, Protestant outlets overwhelmingly dominated Christian media. While Bishop Fulton Sheen utilized television to teach the faith, the rise in popularity of Billy Graham, coupled with the boom in televangelism (including but not limited to the scandalous Jimmy Swaggart and Jim and Tammy Faye Bakker) far outrivaled Catholic influence in this sphere until the founding and growth of EWTN.

Rita Antoinette Rizzo, better known to American Catholics as Mother Angelica, founded EWTN, touted as the world's largest religious media network[5] in the early 1980s in a garage studio in a monastery in Alabama.[6]

Nearly a decade after professing solemn vows as a Poor Clare of Perpetual Adoration, Rizzo, who took the religious name Sister Mary Angelica, realized a desire to establish a monastery in the Bible Belt of the southern United States to attract Black people to the Church amid the civil rights movement.[7] She was particularly motivated to recruit Black women to become contemplative nuns.[8] She acknowledged the insults and persecution heaped onto the Black community, whom she recognized as "a people dear to the Heart of God."[9] In 1961, Mother Angelica founded Our Lady of the Angels Monastery in Ironsdale, Alabama, a community with a Catholic population of 2 percent.[10] In 1962, she began recording talks on the Catholic faith, marking the beginning of her media outreach.

In the 1970s she made videos of talks that were aired on the conservative evangelical Christian Broadcasting Network (CBN),[11] founded by Pat Robertson, famous for the show *The 700 Club*. Through CBN, Pat Robertson perpetuated the culture wars during the Reagan era,[12] continuing through the Trump presidency, for which CBN was a bastion of support. CBN's trajectory foreshadowed EWTN's.

In 1981, EWTN was born—the first Catholic satellite television station in the United States,[13] solely dependent on viewer contributions. In the beginning the channel did not solicit funds through fundraisers or phone-in campaigns like their Evangelical counterparts. In addition, it did not run advertising for revenue, and offered its channel to cable companies for free.[14]

Like its foundress, EWTN was born in poverty and dependence on the providence of God. In its first decade of existence, the network was plagued by financial troubles, and by the grace of God the network always found a way out until its next financial deadline loomed. Over time, benefactors came forward who shared the belief that EWTN could be instrumental in "restoring" the Catholic faith in America.[15]

Mother Angelica Live began airing in 1983. This was her flagship show, and she used it as a platform to challenge bishops such as, for example, Cardinal Roger Mahony of Los Angeles on his statements on the Eucharist.[16] It is also where she pushed her deeply conservative beliefs. Labeled a "traditionalist,"[17] Mother Angelica, through a growing cable and radio network that now reaches over 390 million homes, in 150 countries and territories,[18] had a key role in shaping conservative U.S. Catholicism inspired by John Paul II.

In the 1990s, especially after the World Youth Day in Denver, Mother Angelica began an outspoken campaign against "leftist" Catholics. "I don't like your [liberal] church. You have nothing to offer. You do nothing but destroy," she said.[19] Her tirades against the "liberal" Church continued, adding gasoline to the culture wars until she suffered a stroke in 2001 that resulted in partial paralysis and impaired speech, causing her to discontinue her public appearances. A year earlier, Mother Angelica had resigned as head of EWTN and handed the network over to its lay board of directors.[20]

In its beginning, EWTN was intended to address racial injustice among Blacks in the United States and to minister to them, but unfortunately, the network never realized this mission. The EWTN that Mother Angelica founded antagonizes the Black Lives Matter movement[21] and disenfranchises members of the Black community. This came to a head when EWTN cancelled the show *Morning Glory* hosted by Black Catholic Gloria Purvis, after her calls for attention to racial injustice following the murder of George Floyd.[22]

What could explain the disconnect between EWTN's beginning and its trajectory? This can be partly attributed to Mother Angelica's embrace of the culture wars, but the stronger influence stems from the network's lay board and financing sources, and especially the result of large donor direction. While in the beginning, Mother Angelica sought pennies and dimes from viewers, the network's battle with finances made it susceptible to becoming beholden to monetary interests.

Heidi Schlumpf draws attention to a wealthy, conservative-leaning board member, Frank Hanna III:

Hanna is a former corporate attorney who runs his own merchant banking institution, and in addition to EWTN he is heavily involved on nonprofit boards, including the Acton Institute, a conservative, libertarian think tank founded by Fr. Robert Sirico and Kris Alan Mauren that promotes free market economics with Judeo-Christian values.[23]

Dawn Eden Goldstein, once a frequent EWTN guest, documented her research into Hanna's fortune, amassed through subprime credit card lending, which targets disadvantaged populations desperate for funds including the Black community.[24] Hanna used the wealth gained from targeting marginalized populations to donate to Catholic right-wing groups such as the Legionaries of Christ's Regnum Christi Foundation through his philanthropic arm, the Solidarity Association. This entity received approval and guidance from then-local ordinary Archbishop John Francis Donoghue of Atlanta.[25]

Most interestingly, this nonprofit does not publicly disclose its financial information. Dr. Goldstein explains that Solidarity Association is able to bypass transparency per the tax codes of the Internal Revenue Service (IRS) for foundations because it is a religious nonprofit recognized by the USCCB in the *Official Catholic Directory*, which satisfies the IRS requirements for the exemption.[26] The IRS filing for Solidarity Association categorizes it as a "Specialized Education Institution," since one of the schools operated by the foundation, Solidarity School, provides special education. However, this school closed in 2017. Goldstein observes that the foundation has moved away from providing specialized services and is focused on donating to other nonprofits, including EWTN and another entity we will discuss later in this chapter, the Napa Institute.

The other issue, which is central to the theme of this chapter, is Hanna's ability to get the USCCB to include his organization in the *Official Catholic Directory*. By attaining this tax-exempt status, it was permitted to operate financial dealings through the Solidarity Association without disclosure. Herein marks an example of a coalition of clergy and wealthy donors. As Goldstein highlights, while the USCCB decides which entities are included in the *Official Catholic Directory*, the organization does nothing to ensure ongoing evaluation and compliance of said entities.[27] Moreover, Goldstein provides a shocking revelation: Hanna, through a shell company, *owns* the Official Catholic Directory.[28] Hanna's organization, therefore is not only in the *Directory* by approval of the U.S. bishops, *he literally bought his way in*.

One might object that Hanna's educational institutions include outreach to Spanish-speaking communities, offering English language immersion and assistance. However, this does not justify financial opaqueness. In addition to EWTN, Hanna, through his philanthropic arm, donates to the Federalist Society, a powerful conservative group that played a pivotal role in judicial appointments during the Trump presidency and had been highly influential during both Bush administrations.[29] A leading member of the Federalist Society is Leonard Leo.

Leo is also president of the National Catholic Prayer Breakfast, and presented the 2020 lifetime achievement award to former Attorney General Bill Barr. Along with Barr, Leo is a cradle Catholic, and both men are described as the two most influential Catholic conservatives in the United States.[30] In addition to his influence on Trump, Leo has a long record of fundraising for nonprofits and publicly defends the nondisclosure of nonprofit financial dealings,[31] classified by some as "dark money."[32] Hanna and Leo share the same playbook.

Additionally, prior to his involvement with the Trump administration, Leo advocated *against* affirmative action during the George W. Bush presidency. Bush, while against affirmative action, wished to praise the importance of diversity. Leo, on the other hand, expressed that this would "disgust any conservative who thinks this is a matter of principle."[33]

Leo has not only funded the culture wars, but his antipathy for diversity shows itself in a hostility to any initiative, including but not limited to Black Lives Matter and social justice movements, that aims to promote diversity. Money talks and those benefiting from a financial interest align with the positions of the benefactor.

Leo is a member of the Board of Governors of the Council for National Policy (CNP), described as a "secretive Christian right-wing group"[34] that likely advocated for the appointment of Amy Coney Barrett to the U.S. Supreme Court. CNP hosted an event around the time of Barrett's confirmation that included on its agenda a presentation entitled "Exposing the Black Lives Matter Movement." Thus, the logic for the complete reversal of EWTN's initial racial justice calling is clear: *follow the money*.

Leo has also been a guest on EWTN's *The World Over*,[35] hosted by Raymond Arroyo, long-time EWTN personality and author of the biography *Mother Angelica: The Remarkable Story of a Nun, Her Nerve, and a Network of Miracles*. Arroyo is unfriendly to Black Lives Matter and has hosted Candace Owens and Niger Innis[36] on *The World Over* to amplify hostility toward the movement. Arroyo is also a frequent guest on Lauran Ingraham's *Ingraham Angle* on Fox News, where they discuss right-wing topics, including their mutual aversion to racial and social justice.

While several other prominent lay board members and donors of EWTN promote a right-wing vision, one of whom I will cover later in this chapter, I would like to turn our attention toward one of its nonprofit donors, the Knights of Columbus. While Fr. Michael McGivney founded the Knights of Columbus in 1882 to offer charity to Catholic families and provide a fellowship to counter Freemasonry, over time the Knights became a pawn and a financer of the culture wars.

A Coalition of Clergy and Laity against Social Justice

"The Knights of Columbus, which supports a number of conservative Catholic causes, gave $1.25 million to EWTN in 2014, specifically to sponsor its news show. It gave two more gifts of $250,000 each in 2015," reported Heidi Schlumpf.[37] Presently, the Knights of Columbus is a Fortune 1000 insurance company with nearly $28 billion under management.[38]

EWTN network partners with the Knights of Columbus in offering a "donor-advised program"—the EWTN Donor-Advised Fund (DAF).[39] A subsidiary of the Knights of Columbus, the Knights of Columbus Charitable Fund (KCCF), holds the donor's assets, and *another* subsidiary, investment advisor Knights of Columbus Asset Advisors, manages donor assets. This entity accepts irrevocable contribution of personal assets, including cash, securities, and real estate, to be managed with the immediate benefit of a tax deduction. These investments can be donated to EWTN or "other qualified charities."[40] Thus, we see a trend of financial opaqueness and dark money, and here we witness what appears to be a clear quid pro quo arrangement.

According to the Investment Advisers Act of 1940, the Knights of Columbus Asset Advisors LLC is an SEC-registered investment advisor, and one would think that donations from its parent to a network that also markets on behalf of the investment advisor ought to attract regulatory scrutiny. The chairman of KCCF is Sean Fieler, owner and chief investment officer of Equinox Partners. Equinox is a hedge fund based in Stamford, Connecticut, that specializes in concentrated positions in precious metals and mining. Equinox Partners Investment Management LLC manages just under $685 million as of 2021.[41]

Inside Philanthropy profiles Fieler as a "Hedge Funder Who Promotes Conservative Values" and is an "ideologically motivated funder."[42] Like Hanna, Fieler uses a philanthropic entity under his control to fund conservative-motivated donations. His Chiaroscuro Foundation (*chiaroscuro* refers to the contrast of light and shadow) donates to organizations that promote antiabortion and end-of-life issues, as well as to conservative outlets[43] such as the publication *First Things*, the Ethics and Public Policy Center, the Busch School of Business and Economics at The Catholic University of America, and Sophia Institute Press,[44] a Catholic publisher that formed a joint venture with EWTN to publish under the imprint EWTN Publishing.[45]

One of Sophia Institute Press's trustees is Dan Burke, who is also a contributor and executive director of the *National Catholic Register*, once owned by the Legionaries of Christ, which Hanna is affiliated with and is a donor to the Legionaries Regnum Christi Federation, and sold to EWTN in 2011.[46] Hanna has not only donated[47] to Sophia Institute Press, but has authored a book published by them, *What Your Money Means (and How to Use it Well)*.[48] Hence, there is much intermarriage between conservative donors and the organizations they donate to. Here we see the mark of EWTN through multiple exchanges of donated funds.

The story of the Knights of Columbus and its collusion against social justice does not end here, however. The Knights came under great public criticism when President Donald Trump staged a photo op at their St. John Paul II National Shrine in Washington, DC, resulting in an interruption of a peaceful racial injustice protest and tear gas launched at protestors.[49] A local chapter of the Knights in Washington whose membership included Black Catholics denounced Trump's visit to the shrine.[50]

Mother Angelica's impoverished upbringing is another sharp contrast relative to the trajectory of EWTN, shepherded by board members with deep pockets and a mighty sphere of influence. With her resignation, she fully entrusted the network to right-wing influence, making it fertile ground for the promotion of Donald Trump's presidential candidacy among its broad Catholic audience, as well as to bolster his administration. As

A Coalition of Clergy and Laity against Social Justice

Christopher Lamb astutely observes, EWTN is "Fox News under a Catholic cover."[51]

We have observed a coalition of wealthy right-wing donors and charitable entities that impede rather than promote racial justice. Prelates who have served on EWTN's Board of Governors include Archbishop Gómez, former president of the USCCB, and Archbishop Charles Chaput, archbishop emeritus of Philadelphia. As we have already discussed Gómez's hostile attitude toward secular social justice movements, let us turn our attention to Archbishop Chaput.

A rising episcopal star under John Paul II, Chaput has been described as a polarizing figure and a conservative culture warrior.[52] During the 2004 presidential election, Chaput announced "there is only one way for a faithful Catholic to vote in this presidential election, for President Bush and against Senator John Kerry."[53] This echoes Chaput's stance that willingness by local bishops to allow President Biden to partake in communion is a "matter of scandal."[54] To his credit, while archbishop of Philadelphia, Chaput lambasted the white nationalists at Charlottesville, Virginia, calling their behavior an "obscenity,"[55] and decrying the unjust death of two Black men at the hands of police, declaring that Black lives matter because all lives matter.[56]

However, Chaput perpetuates a right-wing American Church, even calling Pope Francis a "liar"[57] following the pope's statement on the Catholic network that attacks him.[58] Chaput remarked, "Any suggestion that EWTN is unfaithful to the Church, the Second Vatican Council, or the Holy See is simply vindictive and false."[59] Yet a series of episodes on Arroyo's *The World Over* with their self-named "Papal Posse" suggests otherwise.[60]

Culture warriors unite to promote their worldview, and a combination of money from wealthy conservative ideologues and power from money-backed individuals and entities along with Church leaders found a home in EWTN to push their vision to American Catholics as well as to an expanding global audience. Through EWTN, the Catholic Right taught many Catholics not to pay attention to racial justice and social movements, and, as will be discussed in part 3, promoted rhetoric that diverts Catholics from the Church's fundamental call to uphold the dignity of all people.

The Napa Institute

Another EWTN board member is Timothy Busch, attorney, philanthropist, and CEO of The Busch Group, which is comprised of his legal firm, hotel management and development company Pacific Hospitality Group, winery Trinitas Cellars, and multiple faith-based nonprofits.[61]

Busch is also involved with the Pontifical North American College (NAC) in Rome, receiving its 2016 Rector's Award.[62] Multiple rectors from the NAC have gone on to become bishops, including Cardinal Timothy Dolan. Dioceses often send their star seminarians to the NAC, and they usually go onto higher studies and take positions of power in their respective dioceses, potentially on a path to the episcopacy.

Tim Busch is on the Board of Visitors of The Catholic University of America, and is a high-profile donor to the Catholic institution, with his name on the university's business school following a $15 million gift to the university.[63] Several wealthy conservative Catholic donors have also contributed to the Busch School at The Catholic University of America. Given Busch's involvement with the university and the forthcoming discussion on his positions relative to the Black Lives Matter movement, it should be no surprise that not one but two icons depicting the Pietà with Jesus as George Floyd resulted in much backlash from a conservative faction in the university and were stolen from campus.[64]

Busch cofounded the Napa Institute in 2010 with Jesuit Fr. Robert Spitzer. Spitzer holds a Doctorate in Philosophy from

A Coalition of Clergy and Laity against Social Justice

The Catholic University of America and has produced seven television series on EWTN including *Healing the Culture*, based on his book of the same title, that explores societal ills through the lens of John Paul II's reference to the "culture of death."[65]

The Napa Institute aims to educate and support Catholic leaders to promote Christian values in the public sphere amid a society that views such values as countercultural. Wholesome in design, a closer inspection of the wording suggests the Institute is another fortress in the Catholic Right's culture wars. The Institute hosts an annual conference at Busch's luxurious Meritage Resort and Spa in Napa Valley.

The Napa Institute's site names Archbishop Chaput as one of the inspirations for the organization, and a quick review of the Institute's history reveals some familiar names: Archbishop Gómez is on Napa's ecclesiastical advisory board and spoke at the Institute's first conference. Bishop Barron has also been a frequent speaker, and his media group Word On Fire partnered with the Napa Institute to host a conference for priests on homiletics.[66] Another familiar face involved with the Napa Institute is Cardinal Timothy Dolan.

Hanna is also involved in an advisory capacity with the Napa Institute and the Busch School at The Catholic University of America.[67] The Napa Institute provides legal assistance to Catholic nonprofits through Napa Legal Institute.[68] This organization includes on its board Leonard Leo and William Mumma, CEO and Board Chairman of the Becket Fund for Religious Liberty, an entity Fieler has donated to.[69]

The Napa Institute is best known for its annual conferences at Busch's upscale resort, boasting of nights with cigars and free-flowing wine from the Busch winery. Event registration costs upward of $2,000, which does not include accommodations at the Meritage Resort and Spa, which has nightly rates that can average over $500.[70] Conference organizers, speakers, guests, and registrants are largely aligned in Catholic right-wing ideology, with conference and keynote topics that promote this side of the culture war.

While the Institute claims its aim is to form Catholic leaders, a price tag that high suggests that Napa caters only to those with deep pockets. Additionally, this "formation" is homogenous in nature and does not reflect the multidimensional, multicultural Church. The Napa Institute therefore can hardly be considered Catholic (that is, universal) given that the entry requirements are wealth and ideology. Based on the criteria of this conference, Jesus would not have been welcomed, since his message encompassed inviting "the poor, the crippled, the lame and the blind" to the banquet (Luke 14:13), none of whom would be able to attend the Napa Institute.

If the poor and the marginalized cannot attend, then Christ would not have attended (see Matt 25:40). In contrast, during his public ministry Jesus spoke at lengths to crowds of people of all socioeconomic backgrounds and did so "without cost" (see Isa 55:1). In addition, all four Gospel accounts reported that Jesus offered a surplus of bread and fish to a multitude who had been listening to his message (Matt 14:13–21; 15:32–39; Mark 6:31–44, 8:1–9; Luke 9:12–17; John 6:1–14).

This is not to say that the wealthy did not matter to Jesus, but a rich person's encounter with Jesus could lead to a call to "go, sell what you have, and give to the poor...then come follow me" (Mark 10:21) as with the rich young man or a desire to give half of one's possessions to the poor (Luke 19:8) as expressed by Zacchaeus. At the Napa Institute, however, there is neither a clear preferential option for the poor nor detachment from material wealth, but an offering of "catechesis" to the wealthy without challenging their social beliefs or the status quo. Rather, the attendees are enabled to feel complacent in their wealth and beliefs.

The Institute could use a portion of the proceeds from the price of the conference to support the marginalized, which would then bring the Institute's mission closer to that of the gospel. Because the Napa Institute is not structurally congruent with this important gospel theme, however, then Busch's free-flowing vineyard wine is not the "new wine" that Jesus offers (see Matt 9:17).

In 2019, the Napa Institute Conference included Senator Lindsey Graham as a keynote speaker, in which he praised the presidency of Donald Trump, observing, "God works in mysterious ways."[71] The 2020 conference was virtual due to the COVID-19 pandemic. Curiously, of the nearly forty speakers, there were only three women, two Black men, and one Latinx person, further demonstrating the lack of diversity and catholicity.

More alarming was the discussion of Black Lives Matter. Parroting familiar hackneyed statements, panelists labeled BLM as "atheistic and Marxist," and one panelist, a priest, suggested "it's probably not about race at all if you dig deep."[72]

In 2021, conference speakers spoke even more vehemently against BLM. Chris Stefanick, who produces a television show on EWTN, made reference to "wokeism" and "a new religion"[73] while he blasted BLM and Critical Race Theory, the latter of which teaches that there are no biological differences among races, and offers analyses to demonstrate that race is a human, social construct.[74] Stefanick has previously labeled *wokeism* as "evil" and "godless" on Twitter.[75] Another Napa Institute speaker, Mary Eberstadt—the Panula Chair in Christian Culture at the Catholic Information Center—attempted to link pornography and BLM as both based in the sexual revolution.[76]

However, the strongest condemnation of BLM came from Busch himself, who stated, "Black Lives Matter is promoting racism, critical race theory (CRT), and destroying the nuclear family" and that BLM is a "neo-Marxist movement, operating under some discriminatory theory of Black Lives Matter, is attacking the American experiment, which is based on Judeo-Christian principles. We need to pray it will end or our country will be destroyed."[77] During that same speech, Busch named Archbishop Gómez as one of his closest advisors.

Instead of seeking to evolve beyond secularism, the Napa Institute's catechism conflates Catholicism with right-wing secularism. When one "digs deep," in the words of a Napa panelist, the crux of why right-wing ideologues and the Napa Institute have a negative reaction to the Black Lives Matter movement is that it questions the structures that promote white privilege and white supremacy, structures that provide benefits to persons including many of the Napa organizers and its participants. The Black Lives Matter movement aims to end such unjust structures, which is threatening to these structures' beneficiaries.

This may come as a surprise to the Napa Institute, but the Catholic Church, including in the words of Pope St. John Paul II whom the Institute reveres, has named such inequitable structures to be "structures of sin" (*Sollicitudo rei socialis* 36). Therefore, the stated mission of the Napa Institute to form Catholic leaders to counteract a growing secularism is inaccurate. The ideologies espoused by the exclusive and elitist Institute are at odds with the gospel as well as the Catholic Church's social teaching. The Institute is nothing but a gathering of wealthy Catholics with a homogenous ideology.

The Napa Institute cannot combat cultural secularism while embracing right-wing tenets. Its members enjoy the socioeconomic benefits of secularism, including but not limited to the social and political structures that promote inequity while not prioritizing the Church's preferential option for the poor, which is countercultural and counter-secular. Hence, while Mr. Busch's wine might be enticing and the Napa conference might appear credible, both are counterfeits relative to the "new wine" and the gospel of Jesus Christ.

While conservative Catholic donors hide in the shadows, the Napa Institute makes it clear that it stands for strong opposition to social movements that promote equality, especially

A Coalition of Clergy and Laity against Social Justice

those that promote racial justice. The money from these donors brings Catholic organizations and U.S. hierarchy into their fold.

A coalition of clergy, wealthy donors, and philanthropic institutions, bound together by money and a shared drive for a culture war rather than the love of Christ and neighbor, promote the heresy of racism under the guise of orthodox Catholicism. This coalition does nothing for the racially marginalized other than demonize and disenfranchise them. In doing so, they demonize and disenfranchise Christ, further dissociating themselves from the gospel message.

Opposition to social justice, including but not limited to promoting the dignity of Black lives, reveals a hidden agenda that is evil and godless, a false pseudo-religion. Funding from undisclosed sources, some of which have been identified as "dark money" that promote a dark agenda, further suggest the dominance of the evil spirit attacking the mission of Christ, and insidiously doing so through Catholic clergy, laypeople, and structures.

This confluence of money and power explains why the U.S. bishops have been divided and weak in their response to racism, and why some take a position opposite from Bishop Mark Seitz's defense of Black lives. It also uncovers the parallel magisterium and gospel that dupes Catholics into accepting the heresy of racism using specious and harmful logic, which will be discussed in the next chapter.

Part 3 also includes how we as Catholics can move away from this harmful trajectory that the sin of racism can lead us into. We must understand the mortal effects of racism, resulting in the abortion of Black lives not just in the womb but outside of it, as well as discern our unconscious biases that promote harmful, inequitable beliefs. Through this discernment, we can, by the grace of God, be delivered from the enemy's snares of the sin of racism and grow in loving Christ in every neighbor.

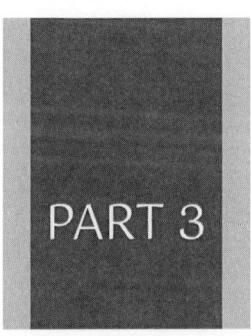

PART 3

EVASION AND ADMISSION OF THE SIN OF RACISM

9

THE ANTI-SOCIAL JUSTICE BOGEYMEN

"Marxist" and "in Conflict with Church Teaching"

Opponents of social justice movements continue to use the same script as they did during the 1960s. During the Civil Rights Era, the efforts of Dr. Martin Luther King Jr. were labeled as "Marxist," not unlike the quotes from Napa Institute cofounder Timothy Busch and several others on the Catholic Right toward the Black Lives Matter movement.

"You can claim someone is a communist and that means they are anti-America and you can completely write off their claims as anti-American....To be communist is to be an atheist. You don't believe in God. And what that did for Martin Luther King was rob him of any kind of moral authority. To say he was a communist, that was to say he was immoral,"[1] noted Lerone Martin, a professor at Washington University in St. Louis who is writing a book on the FBI's smear campaign against Dr. King.

Fast forward, antisocial justice advocates slander those working for justice using this same slur. It's a repeated tactic in the playbook of those who are against racial justice. There are those who would uphold the justification of the Marxist slur toward the BLM movement, stating that the BLM Global Network cofounders defined themselves as "trained Marxists" from the beginning.

As Dr. Sam Rocha uncovers, the basis for this is a short and hesitant response in a 2015 video interview with a Black journalist, Jared Ball, who was challenging Patrisse Cullors and Alicia Garza over their experience and ability to bring the BLM movement to fruition while the Occupy movement seemed to flounder. Dr. Rocha notes the exact quote from Cullors: "'We, uh, are trained Marxists' is not a strong identification. Instead, it is a demand for respect, trust, and credibility from their activist elders while, at the same time, pivoting away from the previous generation's demand for ideological clarity."[2]

The inference that the movement is inherently Marxist, based on a video clip taken out of context, is unhelpful. A more mature and cogent critique of BLM should begin with its mission statement:

> #BlackLivesMatter was founded in 2013 in response to the acquittal of Trayvon Martin's murderer. Black Lives Matter Global Network Foundation, Inc. is a global organization in the US, UK, and Canada, whose mission is to eradicate white supremacy and build local power to intervene in violence inflicted on Black communities by the state and vigilantes. By combating and countering acts of violence, creating space for Black imagination and innovation, and centering Black joy, we are winning immediate improvements in our lives.[3]

Based on this mission statement, if one has issue with BLM, it is because one has issue with dismantling white supremacy and anti-Blackness. It proclaims itself a movement centered on promoting Black joy; one who is against this movement is also against this promotion of joy.

In addition to those attempting to discredit BLM by labeling it as Marxist, there are others such as Bishop Daly who claim it is anti-Catholic because it is against the Church's teachings on marriage and family, including but not limited to calls to deemphasize the traditional nuclear family and promote a pro-choice, LGBTQ agenda. Regarding the "nuclear family," a more multicultural understanding of the family is multigenerational and includes a village mentality.

While some of the pro-choice, LGBTQ stances of the movement are against Church teachings, if full alignment with Church teachings is the litmus test, then a Catholic could not be a Republican due to the party's stances on the death penalty and migration. Right-wing rhetoric offers paper-thin logic in defense of its positions, emotionally charged ideologies seeking to protect white fragility.

"All Lives Matter"

We have all heard the counter to BLM that "All Lives Matter." To give the All Lives Matter (ALM) camp the benefit of the doubt, some in it are confused, and their insistence on "All Lives" might be tempered once they gain a proper understanding of BLM. However, the majority of the ALM camp adheres to this battle cry to silence the defense of Black Lives. If one honestly believes that All Lives Matter, then there should be no conflict in supporting BLM. In fact, such advocates would be busy marching for Black Lives, seeking equity for Latinx people (including those seeking asylum in the United States), defending Asians against racial slurs, and fighting against the Muslim immigration ban. One who truly advocates that All Lives Matter would be an *antiracist*.

In *How to Be an Antiracist*, Ibram X. Kendi defines antiracism as a powerful collection of policies that lead to racial equity and are substantiated by the idea that all races are equal amid their apparent differences.[4] Interestingly, those who support BLM often also work for justice for all marginalized races, not just for Black people. To be antiracist is to assert that no race is superior, no race is inferior, and all races are equal. Every person regardless of race ought to have an equal seat at the society's table.

ALM proponents are part of the problem, not the solution, when it comes to racial justice, particularly for Black people. Additionally, those who militate against the BLM slogan, including those in the ALM camp, may be motivated by inherently racist beliefs. BLM conflicts with a white supremacist framework, or more directly a belief that Black people are inferior. Those who subscribe to these beliefs have not named their racism, are overtly racists, or do not believe such beliefs constitute racism.

Based on the evidence that most of the proponents of ALM are not working for broad racial equity, the ALM argument is a form of gaslighting, a means of creating a power imbalance by making others question their reality. The ALM counter-slogan wears down the BLM supporter by this circular logic, and it can make the BLM supporter appear in the wrong as well as create confusion, the rotten fruits of gaslighting. Additionally, consistent with gaslighting, ALM supporters' actions do not match their words. If they honestly believed All Lives Matter, then ALM supporters should have no problem supporting Black Lives, in addition to other marginalized races.

Gaslighting with respect to ALM has the objective of projecting, which promotes the falsehood that the BLM supporter is racist and only cares about Black Lives, when the ALM supporter is the covert racist, exhibiting no concern for Black Lives, and likely having no concern for other minorities. Lastly, ALM gaslighting aims to divide, aligning bystanders against BLM supporters using its confusing logic.

In defusing and unmasking ALM, it is important to understand BLM. Alicia Garza, one of the three cofounders of the Black Lives Matter movement, originated the BLM slogan[5] following the murder of Trayvon Martin, whose only crime was being a Black in a white neighborhood. BLM is about defending Black Lives from unwarranted, criminal, and sinful measures. Those who are against BLM are in favor of these measures and are racially motivated for Black Lives to continue to experience injustice.

Whether the ALM proponent has a religious or secular motivation, a review of St. Ignatius of Loyola's counsel on the false spirit from the Spiritual Exercises is in order. The evil spirit operates as an "Angel of Light" (Spiritual Exercises, 332) who offers "holy and pious thoughts that are wholly in conformity with the sanctity of the soul," until this Angel of Light endeavors "little by little to end by drawing the soul into his hidden snares and designs."

The good and holy thought in this example, being in favor of "all lives," is used as a cover to diminish the importance of Black Lives, thereby promoting the sin of racism rather than opposing it. Let us not be caught in the fog of the ALM gaslight, but rather adhere to the principles of discernment as well as Jesus's call to love our neighbor by defending the marginalized and disarming the tactics of deception so that we as a Church may emphatically proclaim that Black Lives Matter.

"Blue Lives Matter"/"Back the Badge"

Amid the growth in the Black Lives Matter movement and the protests related to the murders of George Floyd and Breonna Taylor, among others, there has been a growing counterprotest movement centered around the police force with slogans such as "Blue Lives Matter" and "Back the Badge."

There is a false dichotomy that supporting Black Lives Matter along with calling for police accountability equates to a lack of appreciation for the service and sacrifice of law enforcement agents. Similar to religious leaders and politicians, police officers cannot be held above scrutiny. Where there is abuse of power and scandal in any of these departments, transparency, accountability, and justice must be prioritized. Corrupt officials must be punished.

I have gotten to know many police officers over the years. Individually these persons strive to offer their service with integrity. Several of these police officers have complained to me about the pressures they are experiencing with additional levels of scrutiny coupled with a decline in the police budget. As a result, there are departments that are understaffed. Thus, I aim to tackle this issue without unilaterally demonizing law enforcement, while maintaining that accountability and justice must not be compromised.

Do police officers' lives matter? Yes, but "blue lives" do not receive preferential treatment over Black or any other lives. One can oppose police brutality while not attacking law enforcement. All their lives matter. When members of the police are murdered, their family members often receive closure in the court system. However, this is not the case for Black lives. The verdict on Breonna Taylor's murder speaks to this, as does that following the Rodney King trial. America has a long history of favoring "Blue Lives" over Black lives.

Some say, "Of course the murder of George Floyd was wrong; the majority of police officers agree to this," as Cardinal Dolan stated in his op-ed. If police officers agree that what happened to George Floyd was wrong and shouldn't happen again, a Blue Lives Matter rally is unnecessary. Rather, there ought to be a public rally for police atonement. Police and their supporters nationwide ought to publicly and collectively denounce the wrongs done to George Floyd, Philando Castile, Michael Brown, and Eric Garner, among so many others; admit the officers involved committed an injustice; and seek forgiveness.

Additionally, police forces ought to make public restitution by committing to antiracism through ongoing training as well as accept punitive penalties for future actions committed against BIPOC (Black, Indigenous, and People of Color) lives, but Blue Lives Matter and Back the Badge rallies do not incorporate any of these elements. There is no admission of wrongdoing but a focus on the victimhood of police officers.

Here is the post-George Floyd trajectory:

1. A police officer murdered George Floyd.
2. People took to the streets to protest the murder of George Floyd.
3. Some protestors called for the defunding of police departments.
4. In response to both the death of George Floyd and the call for defunding the police, out of fear especially of the latter, some counter-protestors organized rallies supporting police officers with the Blue Lives Matter or Back the Badge slogans.

Supporting police officers so they can evade justice is simply wrong. Police officers, as all people, ought to be held accountable for their actions. One might argue that police officers ought to be held to a higher standard given their role to uphold the law and the power of the badge. If Blue Lives and the Badge are ideals, then members of police departments ought to be exquisite models of law-abiding professionals, and any who deviate from these ideals ought to be firmly corrected.

Police forces should deal with bad actors to promote the impeccable image of law enforcement. However, the actions of bad cops are swept under the rug, making police department ideals mere window dressing. Blue Lives Matter, as a counter-protest relative to the Black Lives Matter movement, is inherently problematic. As stated previously, according to its mission statement, the BLM Global Organization aims to eradicate white supremacy. To be against this is to be in favor of white supremacy. Being anti-Black Lives Matter while being pro–Blue Lives is a covert form of white supremacy.

In a tweet, a professor from Creighton University referred to a Back the Blue rally in Omaha, Nebraska, as a "White supremacist rally in Omaha to showcase Midwestern racism."[6] While the merits and diplomacy of such a statement are certainly debatable, based on the logic established above, the professor was correct. These rallies are covert forms of white supremacy, regardless of whether token members of minorities speak at them. They signify continued complicity in and the cover-up of white supremacy.

Unfortunately, Creighton University, which has enacted multiple antiracism efforts in 2020, caved to pressure and issued a statement denouncing the professor's actions, and the professor concurrently issued an apology of his own.[7] Not only do these police rallies exhibit covert white supremacy, but they also reflect white fragility.

Critical Race Theory

Right-wingers make outcry against Critical Race Theory (CRT) and its influence in school boards and public institutions, calling it racist against white people as well as unpatriotic.[8] Critics of CRT often do not understand CRT and attack their own caricature of the theory.

There is nothing in CRT that attacks white people or labels whites as racist. Even Kendi says that classifying white people according to the generalization of being racist is wrong.[9] But CRT makes white people uncomfortable with their history and their privilege. Rather than confront both, they turn CRT into the enemy. Here again we see the same techniques as those used by backers of All Lives Matter and Back the Badge.

"Wokeism"

Woke is a term originating from African American Vernacular English (AAVE), and is an adjective that signifies being alert to racial prejudices and discrimination. Who would take issue with that?

Members of the right have taken this term and created a caricature of "Wokeism" that diminishes the importance of being alert to social justice, and attacks the caricature as being divisive and promoting values antithetical to Christianity. Deep down, the attack on Wokeism is a bait and switch to turn attention away from the need to confront one's role in racism and injustice.

Like CRT, conservatives cannot accept the discomfort of acknowledging racism. This leads commentators such as Ben Shapiro to claim "wokeness is destroying America."[10] Contrary to Shapiro and Stefanick, to whom we referred earlier, being against alertness to racial and social injustice destroys both America and the Church. The former was founded on colonization, seizure of land, and white supremacy. The latter played a role in this and continues to be complicit in racial and social injustice.

As we will see in the next two chapters, we cannot grow closer to God while letting racism persist in our hearts. If we do not discern the unconscious biases toward certain races that we all hold in our hearts, repent, and resolve to live differently, our hearts will remain stone, and we will become less receptive to God's love continually being offered to us.

We need to better understand the trajectory of racism. Not only does it diminish one's value and denies one is created in the *Imago Dei*, but it also gives reason for the reduction in the person's value of life, justifying injustice and murder. Anti-antiracism leads to death, and the spirits of those who drink from this well slowly die.

10

BLACK LIVES ARE BEING ABORTED— AND NOT JUST IN THE WOMB

Racism begins with inequitable beliefs regarding a specific race or multiple races, or in conjunction, a belief in one's own racial superiority. This inequitable belief alone has an effect on mortality because it could lead to the death of Black persons. The Church must seek justice not only for the unborn, but for those *already born*, particularly Black lives that are in danger due to the sin of racism.

To *abort* is to bring to a premature end because of a problem or fault. Black persons are being *aborted*, and not just in the womb. When that officer's knee was on George Floyd's neck, resulting in murder, George was *aborted*. When the police broke into Breonna Taylor's residence and shot her, Breonna's life was *aborted*.

Black lives are being ended prematurely. Their lives are treated as if they have no value and do not matter. The message inherent is it would have been better had these people never been born. The diminishment of life is not only by swift death but the diminishment in the quality of life. I referred earlier to Olga Segura's reporting on how Black and Brown people have been most vulnerable during the COVID-19 pandemic. Moreover, inequitable beliefs about Black people, such as the false view that Black persons are "super predators"[1] and thus warrant tougher policing, including but not limited to sentencing Black minors as adults, further illustrates the legally sanctioned violence against our Black sisters and brothers. This not only results in the diminishment of the quality of their lives, but in some sad cases the premature ending of their lives.

Structural inequity that results in disproportionate criminalization of Black people, underfunding of schools in Black neighborhoods, and economic injustice further promote the notion that Black lives do not matter in society. Structural inequity is nothing other than "structures of sin" leading to premature death. An example of the diminishment in quality of life is *psychological*.

In Central Park, New York, five young boys were falsely accused of the rape and murder of a white woman and sentenced to prison.[2] The imprisonment crushed their spirits in those important formative years and diminished their prospects in society following their release. This false imprisonment irrevocably damaged these five young men, depriving them of their high school years and of being with their loving families while subjecting them to the horrors of prison life.[3] As Korey Wise, one of the five, stated, "You can forgive but you won't forget. You won't forget what you lost."[4]

Therefore, the Church in the United States must condemn the abortion of Black lives, and not just those unborn. The path of death for the racially marginalized must end, and the sanctity of all life must be defended and promoted; otherwise, the Church does not truly advocate for the dignity of life.

Black Lives Are Being Aborted—and Not Just in the Womb

The "Mortal" Sin of Racism

The previous section illustrates that the sin of racism has mortal effects. In an interview with Gloria Purvis, Archbishop Salvatore Cordileone, contrasted racism and abortion and noted that racism is an attitude that can lead to slurs but can also result in segregation and lynching, whereas abortion leads to immediate murder and therefore is a greater wrong.[5]

However the archbishop, while noting the trajectory of racism, failed to see that a racial slur—the diminishment of one's value—can pave the way for greater injustices such as segregation and murder, the former being a reduction of quality of life and the latter being the outright unjust taking of life. Church leaders continue to fail to see that Black lives are being aborted, and not just in the womb, and instead concentrate more attention on the abortion of the unborn.

As a Church, we have been tone deaf to the reality of white supremacy and the potentially mortal effects that this worldview continuously imposes on Black people and communities. The tragic and untimely deaths of Black persons—including but not limited to Trayvon Martin, Ahmaud Arbery, Breonna Taylor, and George Floyd—serve as poignant examples of the continuing failure of Catholic Church authorities to call out expressions of racial superiority and systemic racism as sinful, contrary to the gospel, and unacceptable for Christians.

Systemic racism demands a forceful response from the Church in the United States. We must clearly and categorically condemn white supremacy, white nationalism, and white privilege. Church leaders must also acknowledge their own complicity in failing to acknowledge and address racism in our society.

However, we can do more as a Church to understand and address the harm caused by implicit bias and inequitable beliefs about racial superiority, and shepherd ourselves and the world to a more just society. We must understand why racism is a mortal sin, and we must explicitly condemn the signs and symbols of white supremacy.

Am I an Unconscious Racist?

The belief in one's own racial superiority can often elude detection if they permeate one's culture or family. We must make an honest examination of conscience and reflect on our implicit biases, including those that have been inculcated in us by our environment and experiences.

Implicit bias is the tendency for stereotype-confirming thoughts to spontaneously pass through our minds. It might not even be a conscious prejudice. One can have implicit bias even when one doesn't believe oneself to be racist. As Christians, we have the responsibility to take ownership of our conscience formation, which calls on us to become aware of inherent, built-in, and learned tendencies that could lead to sin.

Bishop Joseph Perry of the Archdiocese of Chicago encourages this examination of conscience around racism:

> The place to start, I believe, is in our own hearts and in our own little corners of the world. And the first concrete step we need to take is to courageously examine our consciences.
>
> Think about our thoughts and words, our actions or inactions. Do we detect expressions or subtle references to the inferiority of certain peoples?
>
> Have we picked up conscious or unconscious bias regarding peoples of color or other marginalized peoples from our homes and formative environments? How might this have influenced my worldview

or determined my assumptions about certain types of people?

Continuing this examination, we want to determine whether we avoid the experiences, the neighborhoods, or the viewpoints of people of color. Do I see people of color as a threat, or do I consider them beneath me or somehow making my life difficult? At the extremes: Do I get anxious or cross the street when I see a person of color walking toward me?[6]

Bishop Perry's suggestions are an excellent starting place for ending racism beginning with ourselves.

When Does the Sin of Racism Become *Mortal* Sin?

The *Catechism* teaches, "For a sin to be mortal, three conditions must together be met: 'Mortal sin is sin whose object is *grave* matter and which is also committed with full *knowledge* and deliberate *consent*'" (CCC, 1857).

Some might argue that without full knowledge of the sinful nature of racism, racists are not guilty of mortal sin as opposed to venial sin. I would argue that my point above stands: we are responsible for taking an active role in our conscience formation.

Racism can be a mortal sin, given its tendency toward the dehumanization and death of persons. It is also the catalyst for the diminishment of the quality of life for entire communities. Additionally, we cannot ignore sins of omission and complicity by silence. These can often have effects just as grave as racism in its more overt forms.

We don't often hear about racism as a mortal sin. For many this might come as a surprise. No one wants to consider themselves a racist whose soul is in peril. However, in its extreme form, the effects of racism more than satisfy the Church's conditions for a sin to become mortal.

Racism is indeed *grave*, as it can result in the oppression and death of human beings. Racists, in believing themselves part of a superior race, *knowingly* look down upon their perceived inferiors (or consciously ignore the plight of their fellow humans). This belief stands in opposition to God, who made all of us in his image. Those who *consent* to continue to hold that worldview truly endanger their souls.

Furthermore, the diminishment of the quality of life of any culture of people considered collectively inferior, and therefore exploitable, has historically plagued all societies. The difference for Christians is that we are called to be a voice for the voiceless. Not to do so is to commit a sin of omission.

Make no mistake, silence in the presence of racial injustice is complicity. This can have mortal effects on both its victims and on the souls of its perpetrators. Even without witnessing or experiencing overt racism firsthand, it is difficult to imagine, in our information-laden society, that we could be ignorant of existing racist realities in our nation, but the *Catechism* also teaches, "Feigned ignorance and hardness of heart do not diminish, but rather increase, the voluntary character of a sin" (CCC, 1859). Therefore, we have no excuse not to fully educate ourselves about the sin of racism and acknowledge the true reality and implications that it can have on our souls.

Our Collective Responsibility

In conjunction with our responsibility for intentional conscience formation against racism, we must emphatically and comprehensively denounce white nationalism, white supremacy, and white privilege. We must reject their symbols. We must

Black Lives Are Being Aborted—and Not Just in the Womb

root out any implicit bias and inequitable beliefs that underlie the sin of racism.

When we do not explicitly condemn the symbols, messages, and systems that perpetuate racism, we fail to address the root cause—the implicit bias—that leads to violence against Blacks today. As Bryan Massingale stated in a lecture at Emory University, "Efforts of denouncing racism often fail to intentionally condemn and attack root causes and the perspectives that fuel it. These include nationalist ideals based on the perceived supremacy of one race over all others."[7]

Moreover, if it is to properly form and shepherd the faithful's consciences, the Church must clearly affirm that Black lives are sacred, and that Black lives matter to all Catholics. This is critical today, when ingrained notions of white supremacy are now coming out into the open. Any implicit bias against Black people as inferior is contrary to the gospel.

The Church must also avoid complicity in white supremacy and white nationalism through silence. In another lecture, Massingale describes those who ignore white supremacy as "bystanders":

> Bystanders teach onlookers a very important message: doing racist things is okay because white people will let you get away with it....We create safe spaces for racism to fester and to brew...the atmosphere that says when white people do terrible things, other white people have your back. Other white people won't call you out.[8]

The Church cannot continue to be a bystander when its role in our formation demands that it set an example for all its members—clergy, religious, and laity. The Church can start by explicitly denouncing the symbols of white supremacy. This will enable believers to actively, directly, and intentionally form *antiracist* consciences and to identify and shun the symbols associated with racism. Furthermore, the Church must recognize the mortal effects of the sin of racism, a trajectory that begins with the diminishment of the value of life and can have as its aim the end of life. With the vehemence against mortal sin, the Church must warn against the mortal effects of the sin of racism.

11

BRIDGING THE DIVIDE
A Call to Unity

In his 2021 Good Friday homily, Papal Household Preacher Cardinal Raniero Cantalamessa decried the division in the Catholic Church:

> What is the most common cause of the bitter divisions among Catholics? It is not dogma, nor is it the sacraments and ministries, none of the things that by God's singular grace we fully and universally preserve. The divisions that polarize Catholics stem from political opinions that grow into ideologies after being given priority over religious and ecclesial considerations. In many parts of the world, these divisions are very real, even though they are not openly talked about or are disdainfully denied. This is sin in its primal meaning. The kingdom of this world becomes more important, in the person's heart than the Kingdom of God.
>
> I believe that we all need to make a serious examination of conscience in this regard and be

converted. Fomenting division is the work par excellence of the one whose name is 'diabolos' that is, the divider, the enemy who sows weeds, as Jesus referred to him in the parable (see Matt 13:25).[1]

Our examination of the division in the U.S. Church about racism, inclusive of the Church hierarchy, reflects the enthronement of ideologies over the gospel of Jesus Christ.

Relevant to the Sacred Triduum, we ought to reflect on Jesus's prayer prior to his arrest and condemnation:

> I pray...that they may all be one, as you, Father, are in me and I in you, that they also may be in us, that the world may believe that you sent me. (John 17:20–21)

Given the deep divisions in the Church, particularly regarding the Church's response to racism, I believe that in this prayer, Jesus is especially calling Catholics to become united. And not just calling—*pleading*. I see Jesus's prayer not only to the Father in union with the Holy Spirit, but also beseeching *us* to directly work toward unity. This prayer of Christ, prior to his crucifixion, is an invocation from deep within his Sacred Heart. Without uniting to fight against racism, the Church invites the *pandemic* of racism, which dismembers the Body of Christ.

As I have expressed over the past several pages, for the Church to truly be *Catholic* and live up to Christ's mission, its members, from the laity to the hierarchy, must stand together against racism, an injustice that agonizes the Body of Christ. Jesus calls us to remove the obstacles that prevent us from becoming united members of the Body of Christ. When we allow these areas, such as the sin of racism, to become divisive points, they prove to be idols diverting our attention away from Jesus.

In contrast, the Trinity models the unity Christ calls us to. The divine persons of the Holy Trinity demonstrate a unity through a communion of love as total gift. Division prevents us from giving our whole selves to God. Instead, we hold ourselves back, since the outward division denotes the division in our hearts, and reduces our capacity to accept the love the Trinity offers to us. Following his prayer in John 17, Jesus holds nothing back, as he freely gives himself to die for us. In gratitude for Christ's gift to us, can we not at least honor his plea for unity and work toward this in our Church?

Disunity in the Body of Christ harms us all. It prevents us from the communion the Lord desires for us, exhibited by the Holy Trinity. If we can choose to put aside our differences and work toward solidarity with the racially marginalized, we can begin to honor Christ's desire for unity in his Body that also allows us to share in the trinitarian communion of love.

Division is twofold. We can easily demonize those who are doing wrong, such as promoting and permitting racism. However, our call to mercy must be consistent and comprehensive. We must show love and compassion for the racially marginalized, and while we must deal directly with our brothers and sisters in the faith who do the opposite, we cannot depart from the disposition of mercy. Rather, we must see those in our Church who promote racial harm through the lens of the Trinity.

Once again, this does not excuse the harmful beliefs and actions promoted by members of our faith, but demonizing and "other-ing" them will not lead them to conversion, nor will it promote unity in the Church. Echoing Ignatius's rule for discernment repeated in earlier sections, Satan can use our righteous indignation to lead us, under the appearance of good, to respond with vitriol to those who promote racism (see Spiritual Exercises, 332). In doing so, we depart from loving as Christ loves and add fuel to the cycle of hate initiated by racism rather than offer the Blood and Water offered from the pierced heart of Christ.

Pope Francis offers much insight into the praxis of engagement with those who hold different positions than us. In *Let*

THE CATHOLIC CHURCH AND THE
STRUGGLE FOR RACIAL JUSTICE

Us Dream, Francis encourages us to enter the tension arising from opposing opinions and ideologies. Polarization is not the answer, nor is merely regarding differences as "conflict." Rather, even when consensus seems elusive, learning to view such differences as contrapositions enables us to engage them in "a fruitful, creative tension."[2]

In this passage, Francis was influenced by the theology of Romano Guardini. Commenting on Massimo Borghesi's *Jorge Mario Bergoglio: Una biografia intellettuale*, Mark Bosco, SJ, makes this connection between Pope Francis and Guardini:

> The encounter between Francis and Guardini resulted in the Pope's reimagining of the Hegelian notion of history along the lines of dialogue rather than dialectic. Hegel proposed an understanding of history characterized by perfection and progress. Guardini, however, proposed an alternative understanding of history—one that might be characterized as "reconciliation thinking"—not a naïve, optimistically progressive process but a synthesis of polar opposites into a higher, transcendent plane.[3]

Using Guardini's work, the pope promotes the importance of approaching polarities not as static coexistent entities but as living realities, with dynamic possibilities when exercised with sound discernment. When we do so, neither side is demonized, a process that Pope Francis notes is the activity of the evil spirit. Rather, the good spirit calls both sides to move toward fraternity and solidarity.

However, Bosco adds that Francis "was drawn to the idea of a constructive tension of polarities through the Spiritual Exercises of St. Ignatius. The exercises encourage a person to simultaneously have faith as if all depends on God, yet to act as if everything depends on us. This classically Jesuit position of holding polarities together allows the follower of Christ to be deeply in the world, yet open to the transcendent, to be contemplatives in action."[4] One immediate objection might be how one can dialogue with someone who holds and promotes sinful beliefs such as racism. The parable of the prodigal son (Luke 15:11–32) offers a praxis on how to lovingly respond as God does to the one who is far away due to sin.

First, the parable of the prodigal son is a parable of God's mercy and compassion. Jesus introduces us to a father, representing God, who sees his dejected son from afar and rushes to greet him (Luke 15:20). The son's rehearsed apology does not even come to completion before the father rolls out the red carpet for the son who had returned, and he plans for a grand feast in his son's honor (Luke 15:22–24). The parable reveals to us a loving God who is always ready to receive us no matter how far we have wandered astray, and who eagerly anticipates our return.

In turn, God calls us to imitate the mercy that God so readily bestows upon us. As we have freely received, we are called to freely give. God calls us to recognize how each of us is the prodigal son and having been accepted and loved completely despite our shortcomings, God calls us to imitate the father by welcoming and receiving the one who is afar in the manner we have been loved.

Rather than debate if a person in such-and-such category is a sinner, we ought to recognize that we are sinners. From that disposition, we must be ready to receive the other as we have been received and invite the other to partake in the feast that God so freely offers us. The parable teaches us that the activity of God is one of inclusion, and our efforts ought to be geared toward inclusion if we wish to imitate God and follow Christ.

Shifting to the older son in the parable, we also cannot separate ourselves from the state of this character. We can easily lose sight of how we fall short and need mercy, and look down on the one who has gone astray. Like the older son, we can judge the sinner and express resentment toward God's generous compassion, especially when we lose sight of how God offers this to us as well, but the truth is both sons are loved deeply by their father, who desires to share his entirety with both. Similarly, recognizing both the older son and the younger son in us, God gratuitously receives us and shares divine love with us. In addition, God calls us to reflect this divine love to others, especially those who are far off.

Second, the parable of the prodigal son introduces us to the household (in Greek, *oikos*, οἶκος) of God. The household of the father in the parable includes his younger, prodigal son, his older, ostensibly loyal but resentful son, and his servants, but if the father in the parable represents God, then the household of God is *trinitarian*. The Father, Son, and Holy Spirit are three distinct, divine persons who experience unity in being in communion with one another. The Trinity is a communion of persons—God's community of love—that expresses love through the gift of self. George Maloney, SJ, describes God's community of love as the following:

> The great revelation Jesus came to give us was to reveal to us that God is an ecstatic, intimate, loving community, a circle of inflaming love that knows no circumference, of a Father emptying himself into his Son through his Spirit of love. Such intimacy and self-emptying are returned by the Son gifting himself back to the Father through the same Spirit. In the Trinity, Jesus reveals to us the secret of life. Love is a call to receive one's being in the intimate self-surrendering of the other. In the ecstasy of "standing outside" of oneself and becoming available through the gift of love to live for the other, the Father and the

Son and the Holy Spirit all come into their unique being as distinct yet united persons.[5]

The trinitarian household, therefore, is a dwelling of eternal, intimate, self-emptying love.

The household in the parable of the prodigal son hosts a feast for the son who has returned, a feast of divine, trinitarian self-giving love. God freely offers the sinner the most precious of all feasts: divine love from a God who is love (see 1 John 4:16). The management of the household of God, that is, the *oikonomia* (οἰκονομία) of the Trinity, is symbolized in the grand feast that God offers to welcome and invite the one who is afar.

Considering this divine feast, I am reminded of my favorite icon, Andrei Rublev's *Trinity*. The scene in this icon is inspired by Abraham's visitation by three angels (Gen 18:1–10), and is analogous of the three persons of the Trinity. In the icon, the Trinity sits equidistantly in a circular fashion at a table with a chalice-bowl at the center. The circle denotes unity without distinct sides, and infinite connectivity. The chalice-bowl symbolizes communion and love, as the divine persons experience a communion of unending love rooted in total unity. Thus, the trinitarian household is one without sides and division. The image of the circle, which denotes unity and equality, expresses the communion that God desires to offer us in this great feast of divine love.

While the prodigal son dwelt on what he had squandered, and his older brother focused on his younger brother's failure and his own self-righteousness, Jesus teaches us that both shame and condemnation are not how God wishes to operate with us. Additionally, God does not promote an "us versus them" mentality as expressed by the older son. Instead, God desires to invite *all* of us broken people into the unbroken circle of divine love and to experience inclusion, acceptance, and communion that is without division but complete in undivided love. Note this is not to promote or excuse moral relativism, nor does this perspective favor looking the other way when it comes to sin.

God's way, which is higher than our ways (see Isa 55:8–9), is one that delivers us and heals us from sin by pouring forth abundant love and compassion. God's way is one of mercy and forgiveness, ever ready to receive us even when we choose to go our own way instead of remaining in God's household of gratuitous trinitarian love. Therefore, let us enter the pierced heart of Christ, from which his blood and water flowed at the crucifixion, so that we may be instruments of unity in our Church, even with those who hold racist beliefs and practices.

Rather than harbor animosity toward these fallen members of our faith, let us embrace the praxis of the Holy Trinity, a community of love that is prodigal with divine love toward the one who is afar. Let us lovingly engage and invite into communion those who do not value the *Imago Dei* in all people that, by our reflection of God's mercy, they might experience conversion and learn to see the *Imago Dei* in themselves, a blindness that prevents them from recognizing this in all persons.

NOTES

Foreword

1. "The Price of the Ticket," in *James Baldwin: Collected Essays* (New York: Library of America. 1998), 841–42.

Preface

1. Michelle Ye Hee Lee, "Donald Trump's False Comments Connecting Mexican Immigrants and Crime," *Washington Post*, July 8, 2015, https://www.washingtonpost.com/news/fact-checker/wp/2015/07/08/donald-trumps-false-comments-connecting-mexican-immigrants-and-crime/.

2. Abigail Simon, "People Are Angry President Trump Used This Word to Describe Undocumented Immigrants," *Time*, June 19, 2018, https://time.com/5316087/donald-trump-immigration-infest/.

1. Introduction: A Baptismal Call to Prophetic Witness

1. Gustavo Gutiérrez, *On Job: God-Talk and the Suffering of the Innocent* (Maryknoll, NY: Orbis Books, 1987), 24.

2. The Heresy of Racism and the *Imago Dei*

1. Catholic Charities USA, "Prayer for Racial Healing," https://www.catholiccharitiesusa.org/wp-content/uploads/2018/04/Prayer-for-Racial-Healing.pdf. Used with permission.

2. Henri de Lubac, SJ, *Catholicism, Christ and the Common Destiny of Man* (San Francisco: Ignatius, 1988), 25.

3. National Conference of Catholic Bishops, Pastoral Letter on Racism, *Brothers and Sisters to Us* (1979), https://www.usccb.org/committees/african-american-affairs/brothers-and-sisters-us. The National Conference of Catholic Bishops is now known as the United States Conference of Catholic Bishops (USCCB).

4. Definition of *heresy*, Merriam-Webster, https://www.merriam-webster.com/dictionary/heresy.

3. Racism: The Antithesis of the Catholicity of the Church

1. Henri de Lubac, SJ, *Catholicism, Christ and the Common Destiny of Man* (San Francisco: Ignatius, 1988), 56.

2. St. John Chrysostom, *Homily 65 on the Gospel of John*: John 11:51.

3. St. Gregory of Nyssa, *In Canticum Canticorum*, Homily 13.

4. De Lubac, *Catholicism*, 49.

5. De Lubac, *Catholicism*, 49, 50–51.

6. Jack Jenkins, "'George Floyd' Pieta Stolen after Artist Receives Death Threats," Religion News Service, November 26, 2021, https://religionnews.com/2021/11/26/painting-seen-to-depict-jesus-as-george-floyd-stolen-artist-receives-death-threats/.

7. "Full Text of Dubia Cardinals' Letter Asking Pope for an Audience," Catholic News Agency, April 25, 2017, https://www.catholicnewsagency.com/news/36273/full-text-of-dubia-cardinals-letter-asking-pope-for-an-audience.

8. Daniel R. DiLeo, Sabrina Danielsen, and Emile E. Burke, "Study: Most US Catholic Bishops Kept Silent on Francis' Climate Change Push," Religion News Service, October 19, 2001, https://www.ncronline.org/earthbeat/politics/study-most-us-catholic-bishops-kept-silent-francis-climate-change-push.

9. Edward Pentin, "Austrian Catholic: Why I Threw Pachamama Statues into the Tiber," *National Catholic Register*, November 5, 2019, https://www.ncregister.com/blog/austrian-catholic-why-i-threw-pachamama-statues-into-the-tiber.

Notes

10. "Inculturation Is a 'Necessary Process' in the Amazon, Pope Francis Says," Catholic News Service, https://www.catholicnewsagency.com/news/43548/inculturation-is-a-necessary-process-in-the-amazon-pope-francis-says.

11. Pope Francis, "Participation at the Second World Meeting of Popular Movements," July 9, 2015, https://www.vatican.va/content/francesco/en/speeches/2015/july/documents/papa-francesco_20150709_bolivia-movimenti-popolari.html.

12. Rachel L. Swarns, "My Research Into the History of Catholic Slaveholding Transformed My Understanding of My Church," *New York Times*, March 16, 2021, https://www.nytimes.com/2021/03/16/us/catholic-church-enslavement.html.

13. "Controversy Intensifies Over Alleged Racism of India's St. Francis Xavier," *Los Angeles Times* Archives, December 31, 1994, https://www.latimes.com/archives/la-xpm-1994-12-31-me-14847-story.html.

14. "Controversy Intensifies."

15. St. Francis Xavier, *The Letters and Instructions of Francis Xavier*, ed. John W. Padberg, SJ, et al. (St. Louis: Institute of Jesuit Sources, 1996), 153.

16. A. K. Priolkar, *The Goa Inquisition: The Terrible Tribunal for the East* (Goa: Rajhauns Vitaran, 1961).

17. Nivan, "The Goan Inquisition by the Portuguese: A Forgotten Holocaust of Hindus and Jews," *OpIndia*, September 18, 2020, https://www.opindia.com/2020/09/the-goa-inquisition-by-portuguese-forgotten-holocaust-of-hindus-jews/.

18. Nivan, "Goan Inquisition."

19. St. Ignatius of Loyola, "Ignatius on Missions (1552)," *Ignatius of Loyola: Letters and Instructions*, ed. John W. Padberg, SJ, et al. (St. Louis: Institute of Jesuit Sources, 1996), 393.

4. A House of Divided Bishops Cannot Stand against Racism

1. Andrea De Angelis, "No to Racial Discrimination, Even in Times of War and Pandemics," *Vatican News*, March 22, 2022,

https://www.vaticannews.va/en/africa/news/2022-03/no-to-racial-discrimination-even-in-times-of-war-and-pandemics.html.

2. "Most Border Wall Opponents, Supporters Say Shutdown Concessions Are Unacceptable," Pew Research Center, January 16, 2019, https://www.pewresearch.org/politics/2019/01/16/most-border-wall-opponents-supporters-say-shutdown-concessions-are-unacceptable/.

3. Cardinal Timothy Dolan, "For God's Sake, Stop Demonizing the NYPD," *New York Post*, July 1, 2020, https://nypost.com/2020/07/01/stop-demonizing-the-nypd-cardinal-dolan/.

4. "Cardinal Dolan Decries 'Dangerous' Removal of Monuments: 'Memory and Tradition Are Very, Very Important,'" Fox News, June 30, 2020, https://www.foxnews.com/media/cardinal-dolan-dangerous-removal-monuments-statues-tradition.

5. Bishop Robert Barron, "Why 'What Are the Bishops Doing About It' Is the Wrong Question," *Word on Fire*, June 24, 2020, https://www.wordonfire.org/articles/barron/why-what-are-the-bishops-doing-about-it-is-the-wrong-question/.

6. Archbishop José Gómez, "Reflections on the Church and America's New Religions," *LA Catholics*, November 4, 2021, https://archbishopgomez.org/blog/reflections-on-the-church-and-americas-new-religions.

7. Rob McCann, "Message to Staff & Clients from Catholic Charities President & CEO Rob McCann," Catholic Charities Eastern Washington, June 19, 2020, https://www.youtube.com/watch?v=lKRalTfFNDo.

8. Katy Waldman, "A Sociologist Examines the 'White Fragility' that Prevents White Americans from Confronting Racism," *New Yorker*, July 23, 2018, https://www.newyorker.com/books/page-turner/a-sociologist-examines-the-white-fragility-that-prevents-white-americans-from-confronting-racism.

9. Bishop Thomas Daly, "Statement on Catholic Charities Eastern Washington, the Church and Racism," Catholic Diocese of Spokane, July 5, 2020, https://dioceseofspokane.org/news/statement-on-catholic-charities-eastern-washington-the-church-and-racism.

10. See Matt Hadro, "US Bishops Denounce Racist Violence and 'Fringe Ideology,'" Catholic News Agency, November 17, 2020, https://

Notes

www.catholicnewsagency.com/news/46621/us-bishops-denounce-racist-violence-and-fringe-ideology.

11. Heidi Schlumpf, "Bishops of the United States: The Basics," *National Catholic Reporter*, June 3, 2019, ttps://www.ncronline.org/news/accountability/bishops-united-states-basics.

12. Bryan N. Massingale, *Racial Justice and the Catholic Church* (Maryknoll, NY: Orbis Books, 2010), 45.

13. Dan Noyes, "Oakland's Bishop Called 'Racist' by Catholic Pastor over Black Lives Matter," ABC 7 News, June 18, 2020, https://abc7news.com/racism-racists-black-lives-matter-diocese-of-oakland/6255184/.

14. Peter Feuerherd, "Oakland Priest Calls Bishop a 'Liar' and a 'Racist,'" *National Catholic Reporter*, June 19, 2020, https://www.ncronline.org/news/justice/oakland-priest-calls-bishop-liar-and-racist.

5. Empty Words and Empty Promises

1. See https://twitter.com/gloria_purvis/status/1462122290125197318?s=20.

2. Shannen Dee Williams, "The Church Must Make Reparation for Its Role in Slavery, Segregation," *National Catholic Reporter*, June 15, 2020, https://www.ncronline.org/news/opinion/church-must-make-reparation-its-role-slavery-segregation.

3. Dan Stockman, "Voices of Faith Examines Discrimination, Past and Present, in Catholic Religious Life," *Global Sisters Report*, December 8, 2021, https://www.globalsistersreport.org/news/people/news/news/voices-faith-examines-discrimination-past-and-present-catholic-religious-life.

4. Tim Sullivan and Noreen Nasir, "AP Road Trip: Racial Tensions in America's 'Sundown Towns,'" Associated Press, October 13, 2020, https://apnews.com/article/virus-outbreak-race-and-ethnicity-violence-db28a9aaa3b800d91b65dc11a6b12c4c.

5. Candace Jackson, "What Is Redlining?" *New York Times*, August 17, 2021, https://www.nytimes.com/2021/08/17/realestate/what-is-redlining.html.

THE CATHOLIC CHURCH AND THE STRUGGLE FOR RACIAL JUSTICE

6. Editorial, "B+ for Effort," *National Catholic Reporter*, May 1, 1968.
7. Bryan N. Massingale, *Racial Justice and the Catholic Church* (Maryknoll, NY: Orbis Books, 2010), 75.
8. Mary T. Yelenick, "An Anti-Racism Perspective on *Open Wide Our Hearts*, the November 2018 Bishops' Pastoral Letter on Racism," *Pax Christi USA*, October 31, 2019, https://paxchristiusa.org/2019/10/31/an-anti-racism-perspective-on-open-wide-our-hearts-the-november-2018-bishops-pastoral-letter-on-racism/.
9. Massingale, *Racial Justice and the Catholic Church*, 75.
10. "Most Border Wall Opponents, Supporters Say Shutdown Concessions Are Unacceptable," Pew Research Center, January 16, 2019, https://www.pewresearch.org/politics/2019/01/16/most-border-wall-opponents-supporters-say-shutdown-concessions-are-unacceptable/.
11. Christopher White, "Backing Biden, John Carr Calls Out Political Misuse of Bishops' Voting Guide," *National Catholic Reporter*, September 28, 2020, https://www.ncronline.org/news/people/backing-biden-john-carr-calls-out-political-misuse-bishops-voting-guide.
12. Eric Martin, "The Catholic Church Has a Visible White-Power Faction," *Sojourners*, August 2020, https://sojo.net/magazine/august-2020/catholic-church-has-visible-white-power-faction.
13. Christopher White, "Sojourners Pulls Article about Catholic Church and Race from Website," *National Catholic Reporter*, August 13, 2020, https://www.ncronline.org/news/media/sojourners-pulls-article-about-catholic-church-and-race-website.
14. White, "Sojourners Pulls Article."
15. Reese Dunklin and Michael Rezendes, "Catholic Church Lobbied for Taxpayer Funds, got $1.4B," Associated Press, July 10, 2020, https://apnews.com/article/economy-wv-state-wire-new-york-il-state-wire-dc-wire-dab8261c68c93f24c0bfc1876518b3f6.
16. Dunklin and Rezendes, "Catholic Church Lobbied."
17. See https://twitter.com/dhanyaddanki/status/1293913751800799235 (tweets now protected).
18. See https://twitter.com/DanielJCamacho/status/1292812268024934 5?ref_src=twsrc%5Etfw%7Ctwcamp%5Etweetembed%7Ctwterm%5E1292825550201819138%7Ctwgr%5E%7Ctwcon

%5Es3_&ref_url=https%3A%2F%2Fwww.ncronline.org%2Fnews%2Fmedia%2Fsojourners-pulls-article-about-catholic-church-and-race-website.

19. "Sojourners Announcement of Editorial Independence and Standards Plan," *Sojourners*, August 14, 2020, https://sojo.net/about-us/news/sojourners-announcement-editorial-independence-and-standards-plan.

20. See https://twitter.com/nicholemflores/status/1293618530873745408.

21. Daniel P. Horan, "When Will the US Bishops Address the Evil of Systemic Racism Head-on?" *National Catholic Reporter*, June 10, 2020, https://www.ncronline.org/news/opinion/faith-seeking-understanding/when-will-us-bishops-address-evil-systemic-racism-head.

22. USCCB, "Examining Our Subconscious Perceptions," *Open Wide Our Hearts: The Enduring Call to Love*, https://www.usccb.org/issues-and-action/human-life-and-dignity/racism/upload/examining-our-subconscious-perceptions.pdf.

23. USCCB, "Examining Our Subconscious Perceptions."

24. Shane Claiborne, *The Irresistible Revolution: Living as an Ordinary Radical* (Grand Rapids: Zondervan, 2006), 63.

6. Restoring and Rebuilding the Divided House

1. Michael J. O'Loughlin, "Pope Francis Calls U.S. Bishops to Offer Prayers Amid George Floyd Protests," *America*, June 3, 2020, https://www.americamagazine.org/faith/2020/06/03/pope-francis-bishops-george-floyd-protests-black-lives-matter.

2. O'Loughlin, "Pope Francis Calls U.S. Bishops."

3. Robert Moore, "Pope Francis Calls El Paso Bishop to Thank Him for Anti-racism Message," *El Paso Matters*, June 3, 2020, https://elpasomatters.org/2020/06/03/pope-francis-calls-el-paso-bishop-to-thank-him-on-george-floyd-tribute/?fbclid=IwAR0pPvmtOcwaKilvxjKfzU3_GzATCMCuSpBcvK6CMp8UKxV9HQdekoEUBRA.

4. Pope Francis, General Audience, Wednesday June 2, 2020, https://www.vatican.va/content/francesco/en/audiences/2020/documents/papa-francesco_20200603_udienza-generale.html.

5. Pope Francis, *Let Us Dream* (New York: Simon & Schuster, 2020), 25 and 101.

6. Pope Francis, "Video Message of the Holy Father Francis on the Occasion of the Fourth World Meeting of Popular Movements," October 16, 2021, https://www.vatican.va/content/francesco/en/messages/pont-messages/2021/documents/20211016-videomessaggio-movimentipopolari.html.

7. Pope Francis, "Video Message of the Holy Father Francis on the Occasion of the Fourth World Meeting of Popular Movements."

8. John L. Allen, Jr., Shannon Levitt, and Inés San Martín; "If Bishops Want to Face Racism, Own Your Own Complicity, Theologian Says," *Crux*, August 24, 2017, https://cruxnow.com/church-in-the-usa/2017/08/bishops-want-face-racism-complicity-theologian-says.

9. Olga Segura, "Meet Father Bryan Massingale: A Black, Gay, Catholic Priest Fighting for an Inclusive Church," *The Revealer*, June 3, 2020, https://therevealer.org/meet-father-bryan-massingale-a-black-gay-catholic-priest-fighting-for-an-inclusive-church/.

10. Olga Segura, *Birth of a Movement: Black Lives Matter and the Catholic Church* (Maryknoll, NY: Orbis Books, 2021), 50–51.

11. "Demographics on African American Catholics," Xavier University of Louisiana, https://www.xula.edu/ibcs/black-catholic-statistics.html.

12. Bryan N. Massingale, *Racial Justice and the Catholic Church* (Maryknoll, NY: Orbis Books, 2010), 58.

13. Massingale, *Racial Justice and the Catholic Church*, 57.

14. Dan Stockman, "Voices of Faith Examines Discrimination, Past and Present, in Catholic Religious Life," *Global Sisters Report*, December 8, 2021, https://www.globalsistersreport.org/news/people/news/news/voices-faith-examines-discrimination-past-and-present-catholic-religious-life.

15. National Black Sisters' Conference, "National Black Sisters' Conference on USCCB Head Gómez's Speech against Social Justice Movements," *Black Catholic Messenger*, November 16, 2021, https://www.blackcatholicmessenger.com/nbsc-gomez-statement/.

16. "Governor Signs Bruce's Beach Bill in Move to Transfer Seized Property to Black Owners' Family," NBC 4 News Los Angeles,

Notes

September 30, 2021, https://www.nbclosangeles.com/news/local/governor-gavin-newsom-bruces-beach-bill-manhattan-beach-willa-charles-bruce-black-descendants-resort/2703972/.

17. "Bruce's Beach to Be Returned to Black Family 100 Years after City 'Used the Law to Steal It,'" *The Guardian*, October 1, 2021, https://www.theguardian.com/us-news/2021/oct/01/bruces-beach-returned-100-years-california.

18. Elka Worner, "Juneteenth: Justice for Bruce's Beach Founder to Take Effort Nationally," *Easy Reader News*, June 10, 2021, https://easyreadernews.com/juneteenth-justice-for-bruces-beach-founder-to-take-effort-nationally/.

19. Liz Odendahl, "Leaders Announce Legislation as First Step toward Returning Bruce's Beach," Los Angeles County Supervisor Janice Hahn Official Website, April 9, 2021.

20. Rosanna Xia, "Bruce's Beach Can Return to Descendants of Black Family in Landmark Move Signed by Newsom," *Los Angeles Times*, September 30, 2021.

21. "1910s–1920s: Immigration, Defining Whiteness," NBC News, May 27, 2008, https://www.nbcnews.com/id/wbna24714378.

22. "Under Attack," Presentation on Immigration and Relocation in US History, Library of Congress, https://www.loc.gov/classroom-materials/immigration/italian/under-attack/.

23. "Under Attack."
24. "Under Attack."
25. "Under Attack."

26. Kevin Kenny, "Irish Immigrant Stereotypes and American Racism," *Picturing United States History*, https://picturinghistory.gc.cuny.edu/irish-immigrant-stereotypes-and-american-racism/.

27. Christopher Klein, "When America Despised the Irish: The 19th Century's Refugee Crisis," *History Stories*, The History Channel, https://www.history.com/news/when-america-despised-the-irish-the-19th-centurys-refugee-crisis.

28. James Silk Buckingham, *The Eastern and Western States of America*, vol. 1 (London: Fisher, 1842), 223.

29. Michela Rosano, "Mapping the Acadian Deportations," *Canadian Geographic*, July 28, 2016, https://www.canadiangeographic.ca/article/mapping-acadian-deportations.

30. Mary T. Schmich, "Minority Status for Louisiana's Cajuns?" *Washington Post*, May 31, 1988, https://www.washingtonpost.com/archive/politics/1988/05/31/minority-status-for-louisianas-cajuns/a686110e-9f4e-4f56-a7ba-4cbc8abdef72/.

31. Roy Reed, "Louisiana's Cajuns, a Minority with Power," *New York Times*, May 9, 1972, https://www.nytimes.com/1972/05/09/archives/louisianas-cajuns-a-minority-with-power.html.

32. Brando Simeo Strakey, "White Immigrants Weren't Always Considered White—And Acceptable," *The Undefeated*, February 10, 2017, https://theundefeated.com/features/white-immigrants-werent-always-considered-white-and-acceptable/.

33. Marco Tabellini and Vicky Fouka, "From Immigrants to Americans: Race and Assimilation During the Great Migration," *Oxford University Press*, September 23, 2021, https://blog.oup.com/2021/09/from-immigrants-to-americans-race-and-assimilation-during-the-great-migration/.

34. "Archbishop Wilton Gregory Issues Statement on Planned Presidential Visit," The Roman Catholic Archdiocese of Washington, June 2, 2020, https://adw.org/news/archbishop-wilton-gregory-issues-statement-on-planned-presidential-visit/.

35. Tom Gjelten, "Peaceful Protesters Tear-Gassed to Clear Way for Trump Church Photo-Op," National Public Radio, June 1, 2020, https://www.npr.org/2020/06/01/867532070/trumps-unannounced-church-visit-angers-church-officials.

36. Doina Chiacu, "Senator Warren, Mocked by Trump as 'Pocahontas,' Says DNA Test Backs Her Ancestry," Reuters, October 15, 2018, https://www.reuters.com/article/us-usa-politics-warren/senator-warren-mocked-by-trump-as-pocahontas-says-dna-test-backs-her-ancestry-idUSKCN1MP1I0.

37. "President Trump Calls Coronavirus 'Kung Flu,'" BBC News, June 24, 2020, https://www.bbc.com/news/av/world-us-canada-53173436.

38. Dara Lind, "Donald Trump Proposes 'Total and Complete Shutdown of Muslims Entering the United States,'" *Vox*, December 7, 2015, https://www.vox.com/2015/12/7/9867900/donald-trump-muslims.

Notes

39. Matthew Yglesias, "Donald Trump Versus the NFL, Explained," *Vox*, September 25, 2017, https://www.vox.com/policy-and-politics/2017/9/25/16360264/donald-trump-colin-kaepernick.

40. Stuti Mishra, "Trump Accused of Racist Slur During Debate for Calling India and China 'Filthy,'" *Independent*, October 23, 2020, https://www.independent.co.uk/news/world/americas/us-election-2020/trump-racism-presidential-debate-india-filthy-china-air-quality-pollution-b1243905.html.

41. Emma Dumain, "A Day Later, Lindsey Graham Breaks Public Silence on Trump's 'Shithole' Remarks," McClatchy DC Bureau, January 12, 2018, https://www.mcclatchydc.com/news/politics-government/congress/article194434204.html.

42. German Lopez, "Donald Trump's Long History of Racism, from the 1970s to 2020," *Vox*, August 13, 2020, https://www.vox.com/2016/7/25/12270880/donald-trump-racist-racism-history.

43. Steven Nelson, "White Nationalist Richard Spencer Thanks Trump for 'Defending the Truth' on Charlottesville," *Washington Examiner*, August 15, 2017, https://www.washingtonexaminer.com/tag/donald-trump?source=%2Fwhite-nationalist-richard-spencer-thanks-trump-for-defending-the-truth-on-charlottesville.

44. Sheera Frenkel and Annie Karni, "Proud Boys Celebrate Trump's 'Stand By' Remark About Them at the Debate," *New York Times*, January 20, 2021, https://www.nytimes.com/2020/09/29/us/trump-proud-boys-biden.html.

45. Eric Martin, "The Catholic Church Has a Visible White-Power Faction," *Sojourners*, August 2020, https://sojo.net/magazine/august-2020/catholic-church-has-visible-white-power-faction.

46. Joseph Zeballos-Roig, "Steve King Questioned if There Would Be People Left on Earth without 'Rape and Incest.' Here Are His Most Disturbing Comments," *Business Insider*, August 15, 2019, https://www.businessinsider.com/here-are-seven-of-steve-kings-most-disturbing-comments-2019-8.

47. Matt Hadro, "Trump, Barr, Barron Speak at National Catholic Prayer Breakfast," Catholic News Agency, September 23, 2020, https://www.catholicnewsagency.com/news/45944/trump-barr-barron-speak-at-national-catholic-prayer-breakfast.

48. Caitlyn Oprysko, "Barr: 'I Don't Think There Are 2 Justice Systems' for Black and White Americans," *Politico*, September 2, 2020, https://www.politico.com/news/2020/09/02/barr-race-justice-system-407929.

49. Muri Assuncao, "Wisconsin Priest Who Called Pandemic Restrictions 'Nazi-esque' and Said Democrats Would Burn in Hell Removed from Ministry," *New York Daily News*, July 10, 2021, https://www.nydailynews.com/news/national/ny-wisconsin-priest-removed-ministry-pandemic-restrictions-nazi-esque-dems-burn-20210710-wgff7fpoqfd3lplrudnup6caey-story.html.

50. Rebecca Hamilton, "La Crosse, Wisconsin Catholic Priest Belittles Lynching in Racist Homily," *Patheos*, September 9, 2020, https://www.patheos.com/blogs/publiccatholic/2020/09/lacrosse-wisconsin-catholic-priest-belittles-lynching-in-racist-homily/.

51. Brian Fraga, "Altman, Controversial Wisconsin Priest, Still Speaking Out Despite Limits from Bishop," *National Catholic Reporter*, August 31, 2021, https://www.ncronline.org/news/parish/altman-controversial-wisconsin-priest-still-speaking-out-despite-limits-bishop.

52. See https://twitter.com/matt_k007/status/1359668333700763649?s=20.

53. See https://twitter.com/matt_k007/status/1470099556905848832?s=20.

7. The U.S. Church in the Third Millennium

1. Aristotle, *Nicomachean Ethics*, 1106a26–b28, ed. R. C. Bartlett, and S. D. Collins (Chicago: University of Chicago Press, 2011).

2. Karl Rahner, SJ, "Remarks on the Dogmatic Treatise 'de Trinitate,'" *Theological Investigations*, vol. 4, trans. K. Smyth (London: Darton, Longman and Todd, 1974), 77–102.

3. "Address of His Excellency Archbishop Christophe Pierre, Apostolic Nuncio to the United States, to the General Assembly of the United States Conference of Catholic Bishops," Baltimore, Maryland, November 16, 2021, https://www.usccb.org/resources/Nuncio's%20Address%2016%20November%202021%20USCCB_1.pdf.

Notes

4. Pope Francis, General Audience June 3, 2020, https://www.vatican.va/content/francesco/en/audiences/2020/documents/papa-francesco_20200603_udienza-generale.html.

5. Matt Kappadakunnel, "Black Catholic Priest Accuses US Bishops of Complicity in White Privilege," *Novena News*, September 7, 2020.

6. Kappadakunnel, "Black Catholic Priest Accuses US Bishops of Complicity."

8. A Coalition of Clergy and Laity against Social Justice

1. Dan Noyes, "Oakland's Bishop Called 'Racist' by Catholic Pastor over Black Lives Matter," ABC 7 News, June 18, 2020, https://abc7news.com/racism-racists-black-lives-matter-diocese-of-oakland/6255184/.

2. Tom Roberts, "The Rise of the Catholic Right," *Sojourners*, March 2019, https://sojo.net/magazine/march-2019/rise-catholic-right.

3. Tom Roberts, "Wealthy Conservative Catholics Are the New US Magisterium," *National Catholic Reporter*, April 13, 2021, https://www.ncronline.org/news/opinion/wealthy-conservative-catholics-are-new-us-magisterium.

4. Roberts, "Rise of the Catholic Right."

5. Colleen Dulle, "Explainer: The Story Behind Pope Francis' Beef with EWTN," *America*, September 30, 2021, https://www.americamagazine.org/faith/2021/09/30/pope-francis-ewtn-arroyo-media-241547#:~:text=EWTN%20today%20Mother%20Angelica%20ceded%20control%20of%20EWTN,as%20well%20as%20Mother%20Angelica%E2%80%99s%20authority%20over%20both.

6. Jack Jenkins, "From the Bible Belt, EWTN Shapes World Catholic News," Religion News Service, January 15, 2019, https://religionnews.com/2019/01/14/from-the-bible-belt-ewtn-shapes-world-catholic-news/.

7. Graydon Rust, "On This Day in Alabama History: Mother Angelica Was Born," *Alabama Newscenter*, April 20, 2017, https://alabamanewscenter.com/2017/04/20/87939/.

8. "Mother Mary Angelica," EWTN, https://www.ewtn.com/motherangelica/life.asp.
9. "Mother Mary Angelica."
10. "Mother Mary Angelica."
11. Paul Vitello, "Mother Mary Angelica, Who Founded Catholic TV Network, Dies at 92," *New York Times*, March 27, 2016, https://web.archive.org/web/20160331093002/https://www.nytimes.com/2016/03/29/us/mother-mary-angelica-who-founded-catholic-tv-network-dies-at-92.html.
12. Tara Isabella Burton, "Understanding the Christian Broadcasting Network, the Force Behind the Latest Pro-Trump TV Newscast," *Vox*, August 5, 2017, https://www.vox.com/identities/2017/8/5/16091740/christian-broadcasting-network-cbn-pat-robertson-trump.
13. "Mother Mary Angelica."
14. "Mother Mary Angelica."
15. "Mother Mary Angelica."
16. David Finnigan, "Cardinal Mahony, Mother Angelica in Flap over Liturgical Changes," Religion News Service, January 1, 1997, https://religionnews.com/1997/01/01/news-story-cardinal-mahony-mother-angelica-in-flap-over-liturgical-changes/.
17. Finnigan, "Cardinal Mahony, Mother Angelica in Flap."
18. Grace Gagnon, "Mother Angelica: A Pioneer for Women in Broadcasting," *Alabama Heritage*, October 8, 2021, https://www.alabamaheritage.com/alabama-heritage-blog/mother-angelica-a-pioneer-for-women-in-broadcasting.
19. Heidi Schlumpf, "How Mother Angelica's 'Miracle of God' Became a Global Media Empire," *National Catholic Reporter*, July 19, 2019, https://www.ncronline.org/news/media/how-mother-angelicas-miracle-god-became-global-media-empire.
20. Schlumpf, "How Mother Angelica's 'Miracle of God' Became a Global Media Empire."
21. William A. Donahue, "The Truth about Black Lives Matter," Catholic League, September 21, 2020, https://www.catholicleague.org/the-truth-about-black-lives-matter/.
22. Mark Pattison, "Fired EWTN host: 'I Will Never, Ever, Ever Have Regrets' Talking about Race," Catholic News Service, January 4,

2021, https://www.catholicnews.com/update-fired-ewtn-host-i-will-never-ever-ever-have-regrets-talking-about-race/.

23. Heidi Schlumpf, "Money Trail Tells the Tale of EWTN's Direction," *National Catholic Reporter*, July 18, 2019, https://www.ncronline.org/news/media/money-trail-tells-tale-ewtns-direction.

24. Dawn Eden Goldstein, "Frank J. Hanna's Strange Secret," *Dawn Patrol*, January 6, 2021, http://dawneden.blogspot.com/2020/12/frank-j-hannas-strange-secret.html.

25. Solidarity Association, https://solidarityassociation.com/about-solidarity/.

26. Solidarity Association.

27. Dawn Eden Goldstein, "Catholic Foundation's Form 990 Exemption Suggests Lack of Oversight," Where Peter Is, January 6, 2021, https://wherepeteris.com/catholic-foundations-form-990-exemption-suggests-lack-of-oversight/.

28. Goldstein, "Catholic Foundation's Form 990 Exemption."

29. Nicolas Senèze, "How America Wanted to Change the Pope," Chapter 3: 'America Against the Pope,'" *La Croix International*, August 15, 2019, https://international.la-croix.com/news/religion/how-america-wanted-to-change-the-pope-chapter-3-america-against-the-pope/10687.

30. Paul Elie, "How Trump and Barr Are Benefitting from the Catholic Right's Consolidation of Power," *New Yorker*, October 2, 2020, https://www.newyorker.com/news/daily-comment/how-trump-and-barr-are-benefitting-from-the-catholic-rights-consolidation-of-power.

31. Robert O'Harrow Jr. and Shawn Boburg, "A Conservative Activist's Behind-the-Scenes Campaign to Remake the Nation's Courts," *Washington Post*, May 21, 2019, https://www.washingtonpost.com/graphics/2019/investigations/leonard-leo-federalists-society-courts/.

32. John Kruzel, "It's True: Millions in Dark Money Has Been Spent to Tilt Courts Right," Politifact, September 11, 2019, https://www.politifact.com/factchecks/2019/sep/11/sheldon-whitehouse/its-true-millions-dark-money-has-been-spent-tilt-c/.

33. Kruzel, "It's True: Millions in Dark Money Has Been Spent to Tilt Courts Right."

34. David Armiak, "Secretive Council for National Policy Closely Tied to Trump," Exposed by CMD: The Center for Media and Democracy, October 27, 2020, https://www.exposedbycmd.org/2020/10/27/secretive-council-for-national-policy-closely-tied-to-trump/.

35. Raymond Arroyo, *The World Over*, EWTN, March 22, 2012, https://www.youtube.com/watch?v=dGigGN7sUuE.

36. Andrew Mark Miller, "Niger Innis: Black Lives Matter Agenda Doesn't Have a 'Damn Thing to Do' with Saving Black Lives," *Washington Examiner*, June 9, 2020, https://www.washingtonexaminer.com/news/niger-innis-black-lives-matter-agenda-doesnt-have-a-damn-thing-to-do-with-saving-black-lives.

37. Schlumpf, "Money Trail Tells the Tale of EWTN's Direction."

38. "Fortune 500: Knights of Columbus Profile," *Fortune*, June 2, 2021, https://fortune.com/company/knights-of-columbus/fortune500/.

39. The EWTN Donor-Advised Fund (DAF), https://www.ewtn.com/missions/daf-96.

40. "A Guide to Your EWTN Donor-Advised Fund," EWTN Global Network, powered by the Knights of Columbus Charitable Fund, https://ccfnj.iphiview.com/ewtn/LinkClick.aspx?fileticket=vKVjZeGNc9E%3D&tabid=730&mid=2540&forcedownload=true.

41. Equinox Partners Investment Management LLC, Form ADV, SEC, https://reports.adviserinfo.sec.gov/reports/ADV/105885/PDF/105885.pdf.

42. Ade Adeniji, "Sean Fieler's Philanthropy: The Hedge Funder Who Promotes Conservative Values," *Inside Philanthropy*, October 2015, https://www.insidephilanthropy.com/home/2015/10/16/sean-fielers-philanthropy-the-hedge-funder-who-promotes-cons.html.

43. Tom Roberts, "Conservative Donors Aim to Shape Catholic Narrative for the Wider Culture," *National Catholic Reporter*, December 21, 2017, https://www.ncronline.org/news/accountability/conservative-donors-aim-shape-catholic-narrative-wider-culture.

44. Sophia Institute Press is the publisher of online opinion journal *Crisis*, to which I contributed in 2021 and 2022. While I stand by the articles I have written for *Crisis*, I do not endorse its comprehensive views and stand by my stated criticism of Sophia Institute Press.

Notes

45. "EWTN Forms New Publishing Group with Sophia Institute Press," *National Catholic Register*, August 19, 2015, https://www.ncregister.com/news/ewtn-forms-new-publishing-group-with-sophia-institute-press.

46. "EWTN to acquire *National Catholic Register*," *EWTN News*, January 19, 2011, https://web.archive.org/web/20110725062002/ and http://www.ewtnnews.com/catholic-news/US.php?id=2463.

47. Our Philanthropy, Hanna Capital LLC, https://web.archive.org/web/20180623161837/http://www.hannacapitalllc.com/philanthropy.html.

48. Frank J. Hanna profile, Sophia Institute Press, https://web.archive.org/web/20180623161837/http://www.hannacapitalllc.com/philanthropy.html.

49. "Archbishop Wilton Gregory Issues Statement on Planned Presidential Visit," Roman Catholic Archdiocese of Washington, June 2, 2020, https://adw.org/news/archbishop-wilton-gregory-issues-statement-on-planned-presidential-visit/.

50. Sarah Salvadore, "Local Knights of Columbus Council Denounces Trump Visit to DC Shrine," *National Catholic Reporter*, June 5, 2020, https://www.ncronline.org/news/people/local-knights-columbus-council-denounces-trump-visit-dc-shrine.

51. Christopher Lamb, *The Outsider* (Maryknoll, NY: Orbis Books, 2020), 94.

52. Electra Draper and Eric Gorski, "Chaput, with Backers and Detractors in Denver, Looking Ahead to Philadelphia," *Denver Post*, July 19, 2011, https://www.denverpost.com/2011/07/19/chaput-with-backers-and-detractors-in-denver-looking-ahead-to-philadelphia/.

53. David D. Kirkpatrick and Laurie Goodstein, "Group of Bishops Using Influence to Oppose Kerry," *New York Times*, October 12, 2004, https://www.nytimes.com/2004/10/12/politics/campaign/group-of-bishops-using-influence-to-oppose-kerry.html.

54. Archbishop Charles J. Chaput, "Mr. Biden and the Matter of a Scandal," *First Things*, December 4, 2020, https://www.firstthings.com/web-exclusives/2020/12/mr-biden-and-the-matter-of-scandal.

55. Joseph N. DiStefano, Kathy Boccella, and Kevin Riordan, "Chaput Calls Out 'Obscenity' of White Nationalism, Seeks 'Conversion' of Racists," *Philadelphia Inquirer*, August 13, 2017, https://www

.inquirer.com/philly/news/naacp-chief-blames-organized-hate-for-va-violence-20170813.html.

56. Archbishop Charles J. Chaput, "Black Lives Matter Because All Lives Matter," *Catholic Philly*, July 8, 2016, https://catholicphilly.com/2016/07/news/local-news/archbishop-chaput-black-lives-matter-because-all-lives-matter/.

57. Michael Sean Winters, "Archbishop Chaput Calls Pope Francis a Liar," *National Catholic Reporter*, October 25, 2021, https://www.ncronline.org/news/opinion/archbishop-chaput-calls-pope-francis-liar.

58. Antonio Spadaro, SJ, "'Freedom Scares Us: Pope Francis' Conversation with Slovak Jesuits," *La Civiltà Cattolica*, September 12, 2021, https://www.laciviltacattolica.com/freedom-scares-us-pope-francis-conversation-with-slovak-jesuits/.

59. Archbishop Charles J. Chaput, "A Little Wisdom from Bernard," *First Things*, October 21, 2021, https://www.firstthings.com/web-exclusives/2021/10/a-little-wisdom-from-bernard.

60. Lamb, *The Outsider*, 90.

61. Profile on Tim Busch, Sacred Story Initiative, https://sacredstory.net/about/tim-busch/.

62. Dan Morris-Young, "Tim Busch, Conservative Activist-Philanthropist, Rejects Anti-Francis Label," *National Catholic Reporter*, June 12, 2019, https://www.ncronline.org/news/accountability/tim-busch-conservative-activist-philanthropist-rejects-anti-francis-label.

63. Heidi Schlumpf, "The Rise of EWTN: From Piety to Partisanship," *National Catholic Reporter*, July 16, 2019, https://www.ncronline.org/news/media/rise-ewtn-piety-partisanship.

64. Jack Jenkins, "Second 'George Floyd' Pietà Stolen from Catholic University," Religion News Service, December 16, 2021, https://religionnews.com/2021/12/16/second-george-floyd-pieta-taken-from-catholic-university/.

65. Robert J. Spitzer, SJ, "Healing the Culture: A Commonsense Philosophy of Happiness, Freedom, and the Life Issues," lecture series, Institute of Catholic Culture, https://instituteofcatholicculture.org/events/healing-the-culture.

66. Napa Institute History, https://napa-institute.org/about/#overview.

67. Schlumpf, "Money Trail Tells the Tale of EWTN's Direction."

68. Dan Morris-Young, "Napa Institute Expands to Offer Legal, Organizational Resources to Nonprofits," *National Catholic Reporter*, July 9, 2019, https://www.ncronline.org/news/politics/napa-institute-expands-offer-legal-organizational-resources-nonprofits.

69. Sharona Coutts, "Sean Fieler, the Little-Known ATM of the Fundamentalist Christian, Anti-Choice Movement," Rewire News Group, September 23, 2014, https://rewirenewsgroup.com/article/2014/09/23/sean-fieler-little-known-atm-fundamentalist-christian-anti-choice-movement/.

70. Christopher White, "Christians under Siege, According to Virtual Napa Conference," *National Catholic Reporter*, August 19, 2020, https://www.ncronline.org/news/people/christians-under-siege-according-virtual-napa-conference.

71. Dan Morris-Young, "At Napa, Lindsey Graham Praises Trump, Despite Administration 'Chaos,'" *National Catholic Reporter*, August 2, 2019, https://www.ncronline.org/news/people/napa-lindsey-graham-praises-trump-despite-administration-chaos.

72. White, "Christians Under Siege."

73. John Gehring, "Napa Institute Expands to Fight the Culture War," *National Catholic Reporter*, August 4, 2021, https://www.ncronline.org/news/people/napa-institute-expands-fight-culture-war.

74. "Critical Race Theory," *Britannica*, https://www.britannica.com/topic/critical-race-theory.

75. See https://twitter.com/ChrisStefanick/status/1381742607492071425?s=20.

76. Gehring, "Napa Institute Expands."

77. Gehring, "Napa Institute Expands."

9. The Anti-Social Justice Bogeymen

1. David Ramsey, "Righteous Martin Luther King Was Slandered as a Communist," *The Gazette*, July 11, 2020, https://gazette.com/news/righteous-martin-luther-king-was-slandered-as-a-communist-david-ramsey/article_aeeb29ac-c3ad-11ea-956e-e7ccd4fb0784.html.

2. Sam Rocha, "Trained Marxists?" *Medium*, July 5, 2020, https://samrocha.medium.com/trained-marxists-22af4461a315.
3. "About Black Lives Matter," https://blacklivesmatter.com/about/?__cf_chl_jschl_tk__=YAD1FaujJ0ss6jvN3kn0e0uqMN1WwnVTKXuyepiVVsU-1640543521-0-gaNycGzNCKU.
4. Dr. Ibram X. Kendi, *How to Be an Antiracist* (New York: Random House, 2019), 20.
5. Monica Anderson, "3. The Hashtag #BlackLivesMatter Emerges: Social Activism on Twitter," Pew Research Center, August 15, 2016, https://www.pewresearch.org/internet/2016/08/15/the-hashtag-blacklivesmatter-emerges-social-activism-on-twitter/.
6. "Creighton College Republicans Call on Professor to Apologize or Resign," KETV 7 ABC Omaha, July 10, 2020, https://www.ketv.com/article/creighton-college-republicans-call-on-professor-to-apologize-or-resign/33278600#.
7. "Creighton Professor Apologizes for Tweet over Police Rally," 1011 Now KOLN/KGIN, July 12, 2020, https://www.1011now.com/2020/07/12/creighton-professor-apologizes-for-tweet-over-police-rally/.
8. Stephen Sawchuk, "What Is Critical Race Theory, and Why Is It Under Attack?" *Education Week*, May 18, 2021.
9. Kendi, *How to Be an Antiracist*, 122.
10. Tristan Wood, "Ben Shapiro Talks CRT, 'Wokeism' During Speech at Florida State." *Florida Politics*, November 16, 2021, https://floridapolitics.com/archives/473284-ben-shapiro-talks-crt-wokeism-during-speech-at-florida-state/.

10. Black Lives Are Being Aborted— and Not Just in the Womb

1. Priyanka Boghani, "They Were Sentenced as 'Superpredators.' Who Are They Really?" *Frontline*, May 2, 2017, https://www.pbs.org/wgbh/frontline/article/they-were-sentenced-as-superpredators-who-were-they-really/.
2. "Central Park Five: The True Story Behind When They See Us," *BBC News*, June 12, 2019, https://www.bbc.com/news/newsbeat-48609693.

3. Emma Dibdin, "The 5 Most Important Facts to Know About the Central Park Five Case, 30 Years Later," *Oprah Daily*, September 20, 2019, https://www.oprahdaily.com/entertainment/tv-movies/a27181100/central-park-five-case-facts-summary/.

4. "Central Park Five: The True Story."

5. Gloria Purvis, "Interview: Archbishop Cordileone on Biden, Pelosi, Abortion and Pope Francis," *America*, November 9, 2021, https://www.americamagazine.org/faith/2021/11/09/archbishop-salvator-cordileone-gloria-purvis-podcast-241805.

6. Bishop Joseph N. Perry, "What Can People of Faith Do to Help End Racism?" *Angelus News*, November 17, 2020, https://angelusnews.com/news/nation/what-can-people-of-faith-do-to-help-end-racism/.

7. Ashley Morris, "A Catholic Canceling of a Culture of Racism," *Georgia Bulletin*, November 28, 2019, https://georgiabulletin.org/commentary/2019/11/a-catholic-canceling-of-a-culture-of-racism/.

8. Regina Munch, "'Worship of a False God': An Interview with Bryan Massingale," *Commonweal*, December 27, 2020, https://www.commonwealmagazine.org/worship-false-god.

11. Bridging the Divide: A Call to Unity

1. Cardinal Raniero Cantalamessa, "The Firstborn among Many Brothers (Romans 8:29), 2021 Good Friday Homily," April 2, 2021, http://www.cantalamessa.org/?p=3943&lang=en.

2. Pope Francis, *Let Us Dream* (New York: Simon & Schuster, 2020), 79.

3. Mark Bosco, SJ, "Pope Francis, the Pope of Dialogue," Georgetown University Advancement, March 6, 2019, https://today.advancement.georgetown.edu/georgetown-magazine/2019/pope-francis-pope-dialogue/.

4. Bosco, "Pope Francis, the Pope of Dialogue."

5. George Maloney, SJ, *God's Community of Love: Living in the Indwelling Trinity* (Hyde Park, NY: New City Press, 1993), 7–8.